Curiosities Series

WISCONSIN
Curiosities

QUIRKY CHARACTERS, ROADSIDE ODDITIES & OTHER OFFBEAT STUFF

Michael Feldman
and Diana Cook

The
Globe
Pequot
press

Guilford, Connecticut

Cover design by Nancy Freeborn
Cover photos: *front cover:* (bottom) John Wall, SMSU Photographic Services; (middle) courtesy National Freshwater Fishing Hall of Fame; (top) © Andy Kraushaar; *back cover:* © Andy Kraushaar

Page design by Bill Brown

Photo credits: pp. vi, 10, 62, 68, 135, 216: © Andy Kraushaar; pp. 2, 60, 81, 95, 101, 117, 127, 149, 154 (bottom): Erica Schlueter; pp. 4 (WHi(X3)12712), 67 (WHi(X3)52556), 90 (WHi(X3)44473): State Historical Society of Wisconsin; pp. 6, 9, 11, 31, 37, 45, 159, 167, 177, 191, 193, 194, 205, 209, 211, 218: Wisconsin Department of Tourism; p. 39: Jim Erickson; p. 40: Patti Brown, DNR; p. 48: Trish Kempkes; pp. 50, 154 (top): Jim Legault; p. 53: George Sroda; p. 71: courtesy Kohler Co.; p. 74: Anton Rajer; p. 76: Clyde Wynia; p. 96: courtesy John Michael Kohler Arts Center; p. 133: courtesy KF Holdings, Inc.; p. 156: Skot Weidemann Photo; pp. 161, 164: Patrick JB Flynn; p. 174: Perfect Impressions; p. 182: courtesy International Crane Foundation; p. 185: courtesy Sampson Art Galleries; p. 188: courtesy Fennimore Cheese; p. 197: Kerri Marshall-Edgerly Photos; p. 224: courtesy Carol Anderson.

Library of Congress Cataloging-in-Publication Data

Feldman, Michael, 1949–
    Wisconsin curiosities : quirky characters, roadside oddities
  & other offbeat stuff / Michael Feldman and Diana Cook.—1st ed.
      p. cm. — (Curiosities series)
      ISBN 0-7627-0622-8
      1. Wisconsin—Miscellanea. 2. Wisconsin—Guidebooks.
  3. Curiosities and wonders—Wisconsin. I. Cook, Diana, 1936–
  II. Title. III. Series.

F581.6 .F45 2000
977.5—dc21   00-044252

Manufactured in the United States of America
First Edition/Fourth Printing

ACKNOWLEDGMENTS

It was a pleasure to encounter many helpful people throughout Wisconsin in the course of this search for the unique, the unlikely, the delightfully strange, and the positively odd. These fine people include:

People with cameras who know how to use them. Erica Schlueter was a fine photographer, an artist with a keen eye for surprises along the road, and a navigator with solid map-reading skills. Andy Kraushaar anticipated this project by long ago photographing just what the book needed. He then generously shared his work. Jim Legault was the same way.

People who know the territory or know someone who does. For instance, although Barb at the Iron River tourism office hadn't heard about the giant twine ball, she thought Bev at the historical museum two blocks over might know. Bev was not familiar with the twine ball but she knew who would be, Joe at the retirement center in Lake Nebagamon. And sure enough, Joe knew exactly where it was and he didn't mind taking the time to locate the spot on the road map, even though Mark McGwire was up at bat and any second now . . . These are our people.

People at historical societies, museums, and libraries. Those at the State Historical Society of Wisconsin and the Neville Public Museum were especially abundant sources of ideas and details on how to pursue them.

Special thanks to Wisconsin Department of Tourism, particularly Scott Thom in the film office and Krista Elias, for providing both photographs and travel assistance. These were greatly appreciated. The folks at Wisconsin Tourism have a way with words—for example, the slogan Discover Wisconsin! There's just no better way to put it, and they'll help you too. Just call 1–800–432–TRIP/8747 or check out the Web site at travelwisconsin.com.

Finally, visitors to *Whad'Ya Know*'s Web site, notmuch.com, answered the call for their favorite outlandish sights in our beloved state, and their response was greatly appreciated.

CONTENTS

We love to fish.

INTRODUCTION

Wisconsin is pretty much the way things should be. If you want woods, you go up north; for the Great Lakes, head east. The majestic Mississippi River configures our western boundary. And if for any reason you want to go to Illinois, simply point yourself south. But make sure to bring lots of change for the tolls, and remember that you can quickly return to our free and well-maintained highways for safaris to the interior of the Badger State.

Already blessed simply by being a native of Wisconsin (and don't kid yourself, it gives you a leg up on the wheeler-dealers from either coast), I was doubly lucky in having a father, David A., who believed that vacations should be educational. Broadly interpreted, that meant that visiting the world's largest fiberglass muskellunge (in Hayward) could be considered a learning experience.

Dad thought that it was important for kids to step on board the submarine in Manitowoc; to stumble across Al Capone's hideaway in the Northwoods; and to realize what one man carrying bricks on his back up a mountain (only slightly more ambitious than some of Dad's home projects) could build— namely, the cantilevered House on the Rock, made specifically to house the world's largest calliope collection (now a destination of its own in Spring Green). The Wisconsin Dells was our Amazon, the Chippewa Flowage our bayou, the Apostle Islands our Caribbean. Door County was our Cape Cod (even better, since there is no Packer Hall of Fame anywhere near Nantucket), Little Norway our Big Norway, and it's a fact that there are more miles of sand-duned beaches between Marinette and Kenosha than on the entire Côte d'Azur. And as Dad liked to say, it's a lot more convenient.

We would make forays all around the state. Dad was perhaps the first CPA to visit many of the villages where whitefish cheeks were a delicacy, as well as the endless number of fishing lakes where bass (the largemouth variety, not Abe Bass, our dear uncle in scrap metal) leaped into the boat, attracted by the cigar smoke. (Dad never actually did fish; he just sat in the boat smoking his cigar, safe in the knowledge that Mother was hundreds of miles away from smelling it.)

We hunkered down into cabins shaped like cement tepees, along main streets that still looked like Swedish frontier towns except for (or perhaps because of) the chainsaw-carved trolls lining the streets (Mount Horeb). We wandered onto reservations and through national forests. We were transported back in time to Belgian, Norwegian, German, Finnish, Cornish, and French towns founded by people trying to cover up the fact that they had emigrated. We ate our way through the diverse

Billboard on Highway 35 south of Hudson.

ethnic neighborhoods of Milwaukee, Racine, and Kenosha, and along the many stops of the Frank Lloyd Wright trail of beautiful land-hugging designs and leaky roofs.

If Dad is the inspiration, Diana Cook is the real heroine of this volume, having crisscrossed Wisconsin's Class B highways in search of elusive cat-whisker collections and cows with portholes in their stomachs (just one of the many options you can get with your cow in Wisconsin). Her travels have not been without reward. Along the way she teamed with a rural mail carrier to win the mixed doubles Seed-Spitting Championship at the Pardeeville Watermelon Festival, and for her efforts she now has a trophy—presented by Alice in Dairyland—resembling the Stanley Cup. She deserves that and more for her delightful investigative work deep into the heart of Dairyland.

I myself participated in the Prairie du Sac Cow Chip Throw one year, but I didn't even place. The old-timers say the trick is finding the cow chip with just the right moisture content, but I think some of the guys just know which Holstein to back.

We hope you'll find this guide to Wisconsin curiosities both fun and, as my father would maintain, educational, and that it will inspire you to pack up the Taurus wagon and explore our beautiful state. And if you find something a little bit out of the ordinary that we didn't, let us know—Wisconsin surely has many more secrets yet to reveal.

MICHAEL FELDMAN

Her real name is "Wisconsin," but everybody likes to call her "Ms. Forward," because she represents the state motto, "Forward." She has a "W" on her chest, an ear of corn behind each ear, and a badger on her head. She left the ground in July 1914 and has been perched atop the Capitol dome in Madison ever since. The badger's rear end is the highest point in Madison.

HOW TO TELL
WISCONSIN FROM
MINNESOTA

None of the curiosities described in this book will do you any good if you go looking for them in Minnesota, but due to what seems to be universal confusion or a muddying of our border waters, many of you may well do that. Don't. It would be a mistake. Minnesota already gets all the attention, what with Jesse "the governor" Ventura and Garrison "the shy guy" Keillor. But Wisconsin is really where it's at, which is, facing the map with your nose pressed to the Mississippi River, on the right. True, Minnesotans and Wisconsinites are pretty similar. They're probably even close enough genetically to mate, although you'd be taking a chance. Maybe they're too close to mate. They claim 10,000 lakes, but we have at least that many that we don't even talk about because in Wisconsin, we think things speak for themselves, so we don't have to.

Wisconsinites and Minnesotans share a common heritage, having been overrun by the French, who loved us only for our furs; then by Scandinavians looking for a fjord to ford and Germans who couldn't cross a creek without wondering what kind of beer it would make. Neither of us are strangers to biting flies, Lutheran circles, garage art, covered dishes, Native American casinos, bingo in the church basement, lawn edging, and what outsiders might take for an unseemly interest in bovine growth and reproduction. We both keep herring in the house, and we both know that lefse is to be held like a cigar and that lutefisk and head cheese are not for the faint of heart. Yahtzee, euchre, and sheepshead will get you through a long winter night in either place as long as there's a brewski and a bowl of cheese curds for sustenance. Sturdy European stock furnished us both, although we in Wisconsin have been stereotyped as being the larger, when, in fact, we are simply big-boned, with the accompanying nice personalities. They say in Minnesota that when offered something, you refuse three times before accepting; in Wisconsin I've seen it run up to six or seven offers, depending upon what it is.

To the contiguous forty-six states, Minnesota and Wisconsin overlap: People are always calling Kirby Puckett the unofficial mayor of Milwaukee, or tagging Fred MacMurray as the pride of St. Olaf's, much to the chagrin of the alumni of Carroll College in Waukesha, Wisconsin. Historically, the confusion stems from the great tree steal of 1846, when the lumber barons pulled Wisconsin's rug out from under the plat where Minneapolis and St. Paul now stand and lopped off the upper peninsula (currently of Michigan) like a giant appendix. Had they not been wrested from us, the Twin Cities would still be

Lucinda wannabes. A Marathon County Holstein named Lucinda holds the world record for milk production. Her total of 67,914 pounds in one year averages out to 22 gallons of milk a day, four times more than the average cow. She lives at Floyd and Lloyd Baumann's Twin-B Dairy Farm near Marathon and is the mother of three daughters who hold equal promise: Lacey, Jolie, and Brook.

Pig's Eye and St. Anthony's Falls and suburbs of Hudson, Wisconsin, where Cray Super Computers got their start despite Minnesota's claim to be "The Brainpower State" (with billboards on the border facing us!).

Why then, given the commonalities, the shared history and heritage, and the fact that nobody can tell us apart, do we in God's Country (technically just La Crosse, but why confine Him?) continue to feel like Roger Clinton or a pillow stuffed with unknown fiber? Are we the former East Germany to Minnesota's former West? Why do we feel inferior even though some of us are living in Superior? Are the citizens of Minnesota's Lake Wobegon more perfect?

Perhaps it's just a difference in style. For example, the dual burghers of Kenosha/Racine, Neenah/Menasha, and Sauk City/Prairie du Sac, Wisconsin, would never dream of referring to themselves as "The Cities," as residents of Minneapolis/St. Paul do. We know for a fact that there are others, including the Quad Cities (which, with two pair, win). Maybe it's the Cheesehead thing, which only recently occurred to us to be an insult, depending on who says it. Maybe it's just the way Minnesotans stand out like sore thumbs when they cross over in their painfully coordinated colors with names like Periwinkle and Sage, and in parkas that look like they've never been worn, let alone to change the oil. Fording the St. Croix is not exactly crossing the Uatuma in Brazil. But in the interests of peace in the neighborhood and upholding the sovereignty of the great state of Wisconsin, here are ten ways to tell that you're in Wisconsin and not Minnesota:

1. People are driving 55 mph in the passing lane. It's well within our rights; after all, the minimum is 40, so we're actually speeding. They raised it to 65 in spots, but that's not our problem. Unlike those fleeing Minnesota to their cabins in Wisconsin, we're in no hurry to get anywhere. Plus, hit a deer at 55 and chances are good that one or both of you will walk away.

2. Speaking of cabins, you know that you're in Wisconsin if you see an SUV with Brainerd (MN) plates backing up a

bass boat to the lake. What with only 10,000 lakes (many scarcely more than puddles) and an average of 100 cabin sites per, there are only 1 million indigenous cabins for 4 million Minnesotans—a shortfall of some 30,000 lakes that they're not going to find in landlocked Iowa.

3. We don't brag about our children's SAT scores in Wisconsin, and not because they don't have them. While Minnesotans may edge us out in some tests, you tell me who the Minnesota Multiphasic Personality Inventory is geared toward.

4. If it's "Come as you are," it's Wisconsin. The knockoff Italian double-breasteds and off-the-shoulder cocktail dresses favored in some places don't cut it here. While the state motto is "Forward," it may as well be "Whatever's Clean." When we say "Dress," we mean "Wear clothes."

5. If people don't go outdoors in winter, you're in the Twin Cities, scurrying through the skyways like gerbils in a maze. Cold doesn't faze us here—that's why we even bother to ask, "Cold enough for you?" It's not meant to be ironic. If we don't get out in the cold, our winter coats dull and we start to shed. If you need skyways, Madison has as fine a web of steam tunnels as you could hope for, and Milwaukee is the Venice of alleys. Up north you can always find a snowmobile trail and flag somebody down.

6. If you're halfway between the equator and the North Pole and a quarter of the way around the world from Greenwich, England, you're in the capital of the northwestern world: Gesicki's Bar and General Store in Poniatowski, Wisconsin. This is just one example of how unexpected Wisconsin can be—from the world's largest ginseng fields in Marathon County to the rumored site of the Garden of Eden in Galesville (where, when Adam and Eve were expelled from Paradise, they went to Minnesota). This book is filled with things that you are simply not going to find in Minnesota: the world's largest talking cow, in Neillsville; the largest loon, in Mercer; the largest six pack, in La Crosse;

The world's largest carousel at House on the Rock.

the largest "M," in Platteville (which at 400 tons would crush any letter in the Hollywood Hills); and the 4½-story muskie, in Hayward, from whose jaws, if your wife gets down low enough to take the picture, you can appear to be dangling. Two can play at this "world class" game.

7. If you show up with your spouse and no one else at a restaurant or coffee shop and the girl asks you "How many?" you're in Wisconsin. We take nothing for granted. If you insist on waiting for a booth, don't block the cigarette machine. Don't ask to see the menu before you sit down—it's not going to change things any, and the waitstaff resents it. If you're here on business, please remember that we don't "take a lunch" in Wisconsin, we eat one, and we'll be happy to chat after the fried ice cream.

8. "Uff da!" and similar Norwegian exclamations occur in both states, but clearly Wisconsin is where a water fountain is a "bubbler" and "Ain'a hey" is the equivalent of "Mon Dieu!" If possible, begin all stories with "So I says . . .," and make sure it's one worth telling: We have very high standards.

9. Wisconsin, the Côte d'Azur of the upper Midwest, averages 2 to 4 degrees Fahrenheit warmer than Minnesota, and 360 degrees warmer than the dark side of Mercury (not counting wind chill), so pack accordingly.

10. You may be able to find a pair of fish cheeks in the land of the Golden Gopher, but fish boils come from Door County, Wisconsin, a fact that so many Minnesotans and others are aware of, it's getting impossible to get into one. So you

Larry Primeau of De Pere mounted a deer rack to a 1960s Packer helmet and became the Green Bay Packalope. Green and gold Mardi Gras beads (recalling the Super Bowl XXXI victory in New Orleans) and a mini-cheese wedge complete his ensemble. He represents the Packers in the Visa Hall of Fans, but he's still number 3,500 on the waiting list for season tickets.

might just want to head out to the deck with a large kettle, half a face cord of oak, a dozen small red potatoes, 1½ pounds of small onions, a cheesecloth, eight quarts of water, a pound of salt, two or three pounds of fish steaks, one cup of butter, a pile of lemon wedges, and a couple of quarts of kerosene, and take things into your own hands. Since this is a potentially fatal combination, however, feel free to call and we'll talk you down—or, better yet, come by the house and we'll head for the White Gull.

A 16-foot, one-ton loon emphasizes Mercer's claim as the Loon Capital.

NORTHWEST

RUNNING YOU RAGGEDY
Bayfield

If it's a cry for help, it's not thinly disguised: Irene and
Richard Radke live among thousands of smiling faces of
Raggedy Ann and Andy—not only the dolls but also their
images on music boxes, dishes, furniture, clothing, costumes,
planters, snow globes, cookie jars, banks, bedding, radios,
towels, nightlights, cookie molds, canned goods, piñatas . . .

A bright-eyed class of Raggedy scholars.

A look around convinces you in a matter of seconds how lucky Irene and Richard were to find each other. Luckier, if they still *can* amidst all the Raggedys.

The Radkes' collection fills the house from top to bottom. The Raggedys and their paraphernalia cover the chairs, couches, tables, and shelves of the living and dining areas. Upstairs (a doll is perched on every step along the way) they occupy all the key bathroom fixtures and presumably use the products at hand—the Raggedy toothbrushes, dispensers, soap, nail polish, and makeup kits. They sit at little desks in the schoolroom, and they nap in little cradles in the day-care center. They monopolize the beds and store their notepaper, greeting cards, Christmas ornaments, and such in all the dresser drawers. Their linens and clothing cram the closets.

Among the posters and art that have been framed is a cartoon in which Raggedy Ann—huggable and homespun, button-eyed and slue-footed—watches a Barbie doll trying on a new outfit. "You're so lucky you can wear anything," she says. "I wonder if that comes in half sizes?"

The collection began more than thirty years ago when Irene, her mother, and her son all happened to select Raggedy Ann music boxes as gifts for the Radkes' newborn daughter. It was a sign from above to go all out, and by now the Radkes have what is—as far as they can tell by attending the annual Raggedys Festival in the creator's hometown of Arcola, Illinois—the largest collection anywhere.

J F K J R . C O L L A G E
B a y f i e l d

A major John F. Kennedy Jr. sighting—possibly the only one in Wisconsin's recorded history—occurred at Greunke's Inn and Restaurant in 1995. There young JFK Jr. met up with several of his outdoorsy friends before setting out for a kayaking and camping trip to Madeline Island. A collage devoted to events in Kennedy's life is on the wall of the very dining room where, according to the room and restaurant Visa charge receipts, he came downstairs on the morning of August 21 and breakfasted on "Omelette w/ extra items, Bttrmlk Pcks w/ meat, large juice."

The newspaper accounts quote Greunke's staff: "I just looked at him and said, 'Hi,' and well, I could have died," said one young woman. "He had lots of hair, really thick hair. And he's very handsome. And he's in really good physical shape. And . . ."

Greunke's is a laid-back landmark of an inn. Rooms upstairs have reading material that ranges from Jack Douglas to Simone de Beauvoir to used textbooks (with your name in them?). There are no phones, no TV, and no "So how're we doing?" surveys. And, of course, there are those omelettes w/ extra items. Corner of First Street and Rittenhouse Avenue. Call (715) 779–5480 for the lowdown.

THE DIFFERENCE IS, GAYLORD NELSON COULDN'T THROW A SPITTER TO SAVE HIS LIFE
Clear Lake

The Clear Lake Museum proudly—and somewhat incongruously—presents Burleigh Grimes and Gaylord Nelson, two sons of Clear Lake who made good.

Grimes grew up on a farm nearby, walked to school across Clear Lake during the winter, played on the Clear Lake Red Jackets, and ended up in the Baseball Hall of Fame as one of the great spitball pitchers. In fact, he was the last pitcher to throw legal spitballs (balls that have been spat upon or somehow moistened to make them break more sharply). Baseball outlawed them in 1920 but exempted the seventeen pitchers in the major leagues who depended on them for their livelihood, such as Grimes. "Ol' Stubblebeard" outlasted them all, frightening hitters until 1934. "[Grimes] walked with a swagger that infuriated batters, and when he measured a hitter from the mound he would peel back his lips to show yellow teeth in a snarl," wrote the *New York Times* in his obituary in 1985.

WOOD FROM WHEN THE EARTH WAS YOUNG

*D*iving in the chilly depths of Chequamegon Bay, in Lake Superior off Ashland, is a bit like peering through a telescope pointed at the far end of the galaxy: you can see things that no longer exist. In this neck of the woods, that means submerged logs from the primeval forests of Wisconsin—slow-growth oak, cherry, maple, birch, elm, bird's-eye maple—perfectly preserved by the frigid, low-oxygen waters. These tens or perhaps hundreds of thousands of logs are what remain of virgin forests cut and floated to mills long gone; in the 1870s and 1880s, these were the stands felled to rebuild burned-out Chicago.

This was timber already old when it was cut more than a hundred years ago—350-year-old maple, for example, of a quality no longer seen anywhere, except perhaps in a Stradivarius. (In fact, some of the interest in the maple "sinkers" comes from instrument makers hoping to duplicate violins with wood very much like that which the master used; if Stradivari himself is preserved down there, they may have some luck.)

The Superior Water-Logged Lumber company's hopes to retrieve 20,000 to 30,000 logs a year from the bay suffered a setback when the Red Cliff band of the Lake Superior Chippewa objected to their removal under nineteenth-century treaties; all future reclamation will be done with the cooperation of the tribe and the Army Corps of Engineers. But after all, the forest primeval has waited this long—it can wait a little bit longer.

Among a great deal of memorabilia are his St. Louis Cardinals and New York Yankee uniforms, a baseball autographed by Herbert Hoover, and his personal license plate BAG 270 (Burleigh Arland Grimes, 270 winning games).

A sportswriter once said, "Let's see, Mr. Grimes, you were from a small town up in Northern Wisconsin, Clear Lake?" Replied Grimes, "If you were good enough, you were from Clear Lake."

Gaylord Nelson was good enough to become governor of Wisconsin (1959–1963) and U.S. senator (1963–1981), and to earn a spotless reputation in both public and private life. The son of a local doctor, he grew up exploring the wilderness at the end of Clear Lake's Main Street. He took his love of Wisconsin's great outdoors to Washington, sponsored environmental legislation, and founded Earth Day. President Clinton thanked him with the Presidential Medal of Freedom, and in 1999 the National Audubon Society named him and Theodore Roosevelt the two most influential environmentalists of the twentieth century. The museum focuses on his career and includes some childhood items.

Of each of them, curator Charles Clark says, "You couldn't meet a nicer guy." The museum is at 450 Fifth Avenue. Hours are irregular. For information call Mr. Clark at (715) 263-2042.

A gigantic pulpwood stacker stands high above the Chippewa River in the city of Cornell. It is 175 feet high and 247 feet long. From 1912 to 1971 it stacked logs in piles before they were floated to a nearby paper mill. The mechanical behemoth is the only remaining pulpwood stacker in the world. The "Stacker City" is making plans to illuminate the stacker after dark.

WHEN THE BEARS PAID
FOR PROTECTION
Couderay

Al Capone was nothing if not diversified. Bootlegging, gambling, vice, racketeering, bumping off guys, fishing. If he had only paid his taxes, he might be here today, in his 500-acre retreat in the cool and stately pine-and-hardwood forest near Couderay. The wily traveler can find it by following the neon sign that says AL CAPONE'S HIDEOUT. In his day, however, this Northwoods pied-à-terre was so low-profile that even Mrs. Capone didn't know about it. Of course, she may have been the last to know.

To make sure that no one disturbed his peace and quiet and fishing, Capone built a gun tower—unusual in the Northwoods at the time—as well as outbuildings with walls 18 inches thick, and a jail cell for unwelcome visitors. Little did the local tradesmen and craftsmen who hauled all that fieldstone in the 1920s know who they were working for. Or so they said.

In 1931 "Public Enemy Number One" had to hang up his fishing pole and head for prison for income-tax evasion—not as colorful a rap as some others that the feds might have pinned on him, but sufficient to keep him off the streets for the next eight years.

The Hideout now has a museum of the Roaring Twenties that includes, among other exhibits, a full-scale reproduction of the Saint Valentine's Day Massacre. The garage (with four built-in gun portholes) that used to house long black limousines is now a restaurant and bar.

Really well hidden. From Hayward (23 miles) take Highway B to NN to N to CC . . . et cetera. Tours from noon to 7:00 P.M. daily, Memorial Day through Labor Day; noon to 5:00 P.M. for three-day weekends through October. Admission charge. For more information call (715) 945-2746.

THE RUTABAGA-FREE FESTIVAL
Cumberland

They've taken the rutabaga out of the Rutabaga Festival. The bland and homely root vegetable—something like a cross between a cabbage and a turnip—is no longer the big cash crop that it was in these parts when the festival started, back in 1932. Gone are the days of the rutabaga bakeoff and the rutabaga cookbook. And if they talk about them at all, they call them "baggies." Even the festival queen is crowned "Miss Cumberland," not "Miss Rutabaga."

Today it seems that T-shirts are the right medium for rutabagas. Festival T-shirts have been spotted in London's Heathrow Airport and in television coverage of Desert Storm. Willard Scott held one up on *The Today Show.*

You can take the rutabaga out of the festival, but you can't take the festival out of Cumberland. The festivities carry on for four days over the weekend before Labor Day, with a parade, live music, a hot-pepper-eating contest, a pancake breakfast, and an ice-cream social. But nary a nod to the humble rutabaga.

One maverick restaurant, Angels Delight, has rutabaga chowder and rutabaga chocolate cappuccino cheesecake on the menu. So there.

The Chamber of Commerce sponsors the Rutabaga Festival. Call (715) 822-3378 for more information.

The nearby town of Boyceville also celebrates a phantom vegetable. Although the pickle factory left a few years ago, the

Cucumber Festival goes on, at least in name. A grand parade, a souped-up garden-tractor pull, and other events take the place of the treasure hunt for the Golden Cucumber or the Cucumber Float down the creek. The festival is held during the third week in August. More information is available by calling (715) 643–2298.

The bumper stickers read REAL TOURISTS EAT WHITEFISH LIVERS because Bayfield discovered that if you stop calling them fish guts, you can sell them to tourists as a real delicacy. Restaurants sauté them in butter, sometimes combined with red peppers and onions or with bacon, onion, and mushrooms. The Norwegian way is to stew them in milk. ("They like to have all their food white," explains one chef.) Gourmet shops sell them puréed in a pâté. Local fish markets sell them straight, for those who want to rustle up a batch at home.

RUN BAMBI, RUN!
Durand

Anna Mae Bauer has had seventeen collisions with deer on the road. "It's not as if I'm out to set a record or anything," says Anna Mae, who probably *has* set a record.

Nevertheless, the intrepid Anna Mae continues to drive nearly 500 miles a week between her home in Durand and her job in Chippewa Falls. Traveling a heavily wooded highway somewhat increases the odds here.

Not all the deer were killed on the spot. Number One (sometime in 1958) was just dazed a little; others have been able to stumble away into the woods.

As a regular customer, Anna Mae now consults the guys at G&W Body Shop in Durand before buying a new car, anticipating the need to match paint and so on. And she has high praise for her insurance company, though on occasion she's been too embarrassed to file yet another claim.

For a while she had four or five deer alerts attached to the front of her car. They were supposed to warn deer of her approach, but the animals leaped into her path anyway—and took the devices with them as they went down. Anna Mae does not invest in deer alerts anymore.

Deer Number Seventeen (December 19, 1998) had a curious response. As Anna Mae got out of the car and approached, the deer raised its head and gazed at her, as if to say, "You must be the Anna Mae Bauer I've heard so much about," then lay down and died.

The Wisconsin Department of Natural Resources reports that almost 45,000 deer were killed by vehicles in one recent year—not all driven by Anna Mae Bauer. (If you're coming this way, the locals advise keeping the windows rolled down so the deer can jump right through.)

MILK

One day back in the 1980s, Governor Lee Dreyfus liked the cheese curds he sampled in Ellsworth so much that he proclaimed the town to be the "Cheese Curds Capital." The cheesemakers of Ellsworth are modest about this honor, saying that no one really makes cheese curds, they're just scraps left over from an early stage of the cheddar-making process.

Ellsworth produces millions of pounds of cheese curds each year. They are not aged—the flavor "hasn't built up to a crescendo," a fact unrelated to the noise they make when eaten. Some people think cheese curds are peculiar, as if eating bland little lumps that squeak is something to snicker at.

You're Cleared for Landing
Elmwood

Thousands of Earthlings, some in costume, come to Elmwood, population 775, for UFO Days in July.

The first reported sighting of a UFO here occurred in March 1975. Something like a very bright star chased a mother and her three children home and tried to land in front of their car. A few nights later police officer George Wheeler sighted "a flaming ball the size of a football field." It zapped his car with a blue light that burned out all the plugs and points. The CIA investigated. Even Dan Rather came.

Enough sightings occurred over the next several years that in 1988 Elmwood announced plans for a $25 million visitors' center—for aliens. It would include a gigantic beacon and landing strip, a huge image on the ground to welcome space travelers, accommodations and laboratories for dozens of scientists, and a video studio. "This is not a gimmick," said the mayor.

The ground image caused considerable debate. The sketch from a local artist showed two lanky figures shaking hands. What if a handshake doesn't mean the same thing to aliens that it means to humans? "If they're smart enough to get here," said the mayor, "they're smart enough to figure everything else out." The handshake stayed.

Elmwood dropped the plan for the visitors' center for lack of funds, but it has an annual celebration on the last full weekend in July. There's a parade, dancing, horseshoe and cow-chip throwing, and of course UFO burgers, buttons, and bumper stickers. Call (715) 639–3792 for more information.

ALL DRESSED OUT AND NOWHERE TO GO
Glidden

Here lies the "World Record Black Bear." It was killed 5 miles northeast of Glidden on November 23, 1963.

Hjalmer Krans had noticed a bear den while looking over a timber tract in a cedar swamp and reported his discovery to two hunters, Otto Hedbany and Donald Streubel of New Berlin. According to the *Glidden Enterprise*, "The bear had been denned for some time and did not bestir itself when discovered. Mr. Hedbany had no difficulty in killing the animal with one shot in the head, fired from his 303 Savage rifle. It took seven men about an hour to drag the bear 150 yards to a car."

Yet another feather in Wisconsin's cap: the World's Largest Pine Log.

WHAT'S TALL, HAIRY, AND DOESN'T WEAR A FAVRE JERSEY?

Although Sasquatch—Bigfoot, to his friends—is most often associated with the Pacific Northwest, someone forgot to tell James Hughes of Granton, a deliveryman for the Black River Shopper. *While on his route on County Highway H at about 5:15 on the morning of March 28, 2000, Hughes saw a hirsute, ape-faced creature a good 8 feet tall and easily 500 pounds making off with a goat under one arm. Since the thing still had one arm free, Hughes put the pedal to the metal and left the* Shoppers *in his trunk. In his report to the Clark County Sheriff's Department, he described the beast as "all covered with hair, a real dark gray color, with some spots that look a honey color. It was walking on two legs, and it was mighty, mighty, big." Hughes feared for his life, but the creature had already gotten his goat. The sheriff, unable to find any footprints or scat, said he had no reports of goats missing, let alone, well, you know.*

According to the Milwaukee Journal Sentinel, *Hughes waited a day to file his report, fearing that people would think him crazy, but stressed, "I don't drink, I don't use dope, and I was wide awake."*

It would be easy to dismiss this report as an aberration were it not for the fact that Bigfoot sightings in Wisconsin have been numerous, dating back at least to 1910, when a large, hairy creature followed a ten-year-old girl home, leaving tracks "twice as large as her father's." Before that a similar beast, the Windigo, was known to the Chippewa and incorporated into their tribal lore. In The W-Files, *author Jay Rath recounts sightings of huge, upright, animal-like creatures in Delavan in 1964; in Waupaca County in 1968 (where a group of hunters would have shot it had it only looked a little less human); in Lafayette County in 1970; and in 1992 in rural Jefferson County, standing over a roadkill on State Highway 106.*

All the descriptions are much the same as Hughes's. Needless to say, to see something of that size in Wisconsin without so much as a shred of Packer paraphernalia on it can only be described as very, very curious indeed.

Granton is in Clark County, about 10 miles east of Neillsville.

The hunters weighed the bear at the Schraufnagel Lumber Yard: 665 pounds "dressed out". It measured 7 feet 10 inches from tail to nose and 72 inches around the chest, and was estimated to be twelve years old.

The bear is on display in a glass-and-log case next to the world's largest white pine log (1,940 board feet). It is 2 blocks east of Highway 13, just off Grant Street.

PAUL BUNYAN JUST GOT BETTER PRESS
Grantsburg

A life-size wood sculpture of a hometown hero, Anders Gustav Anderson (1872–1926), stands in front of the village office at 416 South Pine Street. "Big Gust" stood a well-proportioned 7 feet 6 inches (that's 4 inches taller than Kareem Abdul-Jabbar) and weighed 360 pounds.

Born in Sweden, Big Gust was village marshal of Grantsburg for the last twenty-five years of his life, and the biggest police officer in the country. According to one story, Gust once broke up a disturbance at the local saloon by hoisting a man under each arm and heading toward the jail. At Oak and Madison they asked to be put down and walked peaceably the rest of the way. He was also helpful if power lines needed to be strung or if a car or even a house needed to be lifted, for he was very strong.

Gust was also good-natured. When he died no one could recall an angry or unkind word from him; and if there were, chances are they would have let it pass.

Alf Manley Olson, a lifelong resident of Grantsburg, carved the Big Gust likeness in 1980 from laminated basswood. It weighs eight pounds more than Gust did. The Grantsburg Area

Historical Society Museum, at 133 West Wisconsin Avenue, displays the crutch specially built for Gust when he slipped on ice in front of the fire hall in 1918 and broke his hip, along with other items that indicate his size.

FASTEST SHOW ON H_2O
Grantsburg

What's the fun of having a snowmobile if you can run around in it only about eight months out of the year? Some such thinking inspired the activity on Memory Lake that now attracts thousands of spectators every summer: drag races in snowmobiles on open water, something that usually happens only at bar time—Wisconsin parlance for closing time—when the ice is breaking up.

Three or four snowmobiles at a time take a 20-foot run from the shore, hit the water, and skip across the top, the way a

---

*D*ick's Bar in Hudson serves chicken in a hubcap with soup and salad on the side. Those who must know why are told of a dream involving chickens and hubcaps, "and if you understand that, we've failed." No need to count your hubcaps before you drive away.

Dick's has been in this location since 1860: next to the marina on the Mississippi River, 111 Walnut Street (old Highway 12). Open 8:00 A.M. to bar time. Give them a call at (715) 386–5222.

rock skips across a pond. The fastest one wins—and speeds can reach 65 or 70 miles per hour on the straightaway. Another event involves racing around a series of buoys. Whichever, unless it's done very fast, the snowmobile sinks.

To see it is to believe it. The World Championship Snowmobile Watercross takes place on the third weekend in July. Call (715) 463–5845 for information.

THERE'S ALWAYS A CATCH
Hayward

The Fresh Water Fishing Hall of Fame has hundreds of outboard motors from way back when ("Look! There's Grandpa's old motor!"), thousands of fishing poles and rods and reels, and more kinds of minnow buckets than you ever dreamed of. It's a trip down memory lane of tackle boxes and depth finders. It's also the last word on freshwater fishing records. If you think you have a trophy, have it authenticated here.

But the part that made our hearts beat faster was the exhibit of hundreds of fishing hooks and lures that have snagged fishermen, each one documented by the fisher's name, hometown (Illinois is well represented), and year and lake of snag. It began with the collection of a Grantsburg doctor who started to save the hooks and lures sticking out of people who turned up at his office about once a week for thirty-eight summers. It didn't even have to be summertime; some people hooked themselves cleaning out their tackle boxes in the middle of winter. Other doctors have joined in the fun to build the impressive collection on display here.

Also noteworthy is the wall of "Poor Taxidermy," the pathetic attempts of amateurs that resulted in misshapen fish or mounts that deteriorated from the use of inferior materials. With all the taxidermists in business in the Northwoods, there's really no need to try this at home.

Did we mention that all these wonders are housed in a four-and-a-half-story, half-block-long, walk-through fiberglass muskie?

The National Fresh Water Fishing Hall of Fame is at the junction of Highways 27 and B. Open daily 10:00 A.M. to 4:30 P.M. (to 5:00 P.M. in the summer), April 15 to November 1. For more information see the Web site at www.freshwater-fishing. org, or call (715) 634–4440.

The de rigueur photo op of your trip to north-
ern Wisconsin, for not just you but up to twenty or thirty of your
traveling companions—that's how big the jaws of this muskie are at
the Fishing Hall of Fame. Big enough for weddings.

PULL UP YOUR GALLUSES AND HEAD FOR THE TIMBER
Hayward

f you've always worn red flannels and suspenders and searched in vain for likeminded individuals, you'll want to add to the cries of "Yo-ho!" at the Lumberjack World Championships. Lumberjacks and lumberjills come from all over the world to compete in such events as the springboard chop, hot saw, underhand chop, logrolling, boom run, and speed climb.

Muscular competitors climb up and down trees about 90 feet tall very, very fast. They saw through logs in a wink. They spin big logs underfoot while trying to dump each other into the water. They toss axes all over the place. In short, it's a lot like where you work, only outdoors. Today, of course, all these things are usually done by machine (the logroller can dump a guy in the drink in a split second), so it's a glimpse of life in the Northwoods in days gone by.

This big event, along with other activities and music, takes place on a weekend in late July at Lumberjack Bowl, a quarter of a mile east of Hayward on Highway B. Call (715) 634–2484 for more information.

P.S.: Galluses are suspenders.

To Taxidermy
Hayward

The trouble with most dead things is they don't make you laugh. But that is easily remedied in Hayward at the whimsical Moccasin Bar, which features better drinking through taxidermy.

We're talking more than your usual fetal deer tableau here. We're talking rabbits in calico kibitzing at sheepshead and Tyrolean-hatted chipmunks drinking beer and rolling dice. Things that would have been, had evolution favored rodents

Judge Wolf hears the case

of the badger that jumped the woodcock season

at the Moccasin Bar in Hayward.

and other small mammals instead of us. See what might have been at this popular local hangout.

Folks come for the "World's Largest Muskie"—the world's largest *mounted* muskie, that is—alone, although larger ones have been caught since Cal Johnson fought for this one (67½ pounds and 60¼ inches) for an hour on July 24, 1949. Just a few months later, for instance, Louis Spray caught a larger one and had it mounted too, but the trophy was lost when the real-estate office where it hung burned down. So life giveth, and it taketh away. The authenticator of records, the Fresh Water Fishing Hall of Fame (p. 30), sorts it all out.

The Moccasin Bar is at the junction of Highways 63 and 27. Open daily. Call (715) 634-4211.

MARK TWINE
Lake Nebagamon

J im Kotera has a mighty big ball of twine. He started it twenty years ago, after reading about other twine balls around the country. There are quite a few of them, although nobody knows why. Maybe because they are less painful to collect than balls of barbed wire.

From the beginning Jim has kept track of the size of his ball—"I take a whole bunch of twine, put it in a garbage bag, and weigh the garbage bag"—and according to his records, the twine ball now weighs 18,200 pounds. That's assuming a twine ball wound weighs the same as a twine ball unwound. Along the way he's marked it on door jambs like a toddler. Today it's all growed up: 7 feet tall, 35 feet across, and potato-shaped, since Jim has to work the angles now that it's too big to roll.

If Jim Kotera's calculations are correct (and unless someone has a ten-ton twine ball hidden away somewhere), he has the

AMERICA'S DIARYLAND

Jim Cummings, of Knapp, has written in his diary
every day since January 1, 1952, when he was thirteen years old—hasn't missed a day in nearly half a
century. Even on days when nothing has happened.
And it's not just "Sunny, high of 80 degrees, washed
the car," but about 800 words daily of activities,
thoughts, and impressions.

"It's about the only way I know to honor time," he
says. "Otherwise it's time past, chaos dimly remembered." It also serves as a reality check. Re-reading
entries reveals that things he thought he remembered
well aren't necessarily so. Writing with a fountain pen
in permanent blue-black ink, he fills large red leather-
bound volumes that by the end of a year contain
nearly 300,000 words.

A respected and lifelong book buyer and seller by
profession, Jim Cummings also owns 16,000 published
English-language diaries. He added a special diary
room at his home in western Wisconsin for what is
probably the most extensive such collection anywhere.

His own diary entries are distinct enough that
reading what he wrote on a given day years ago puts
him back in that day and prompts the recollection of
further details. "It's interesting to be able to reclaim
any day that I've lived. Diaries put you right exactly
where you were, fix you in a point as nothing else can
do," he says.

Knowing the past is not the only reward of such
diligence. Keeping a diary reminds Jim to lead a life
that's interesting to record. For instance, a trip to
Spain with his son and a granddaughter is in the
works, and all three will be writing in their diaries.

Jim Kotera's twine ball.

largest twine ball assembled by one man. There's one in Darwin, Minnesota, but it weighs a mere 17,400 pounds and measures 12 feet (Darwinians nevertheless hold an annual festival called Twine Ball Days in August). And there's one that Ripley's Believe It or Not Museum in Branson, Missouri, flaunts as Guinness-record-size, but it was a group effort, as was the 11-footer in Cawker City, Kansas (which calls its August celebration Twine-a-thon).

A farmer in the neighborhood has supplied much of the twine, and now can't find anything to bundle his papers with. Meanwhile Jim built a pole shed over the ball for protection from winter weather. It's located at 8009 Oakdale Road (at Minnesong Road), Town of Highland, near Lake Nebagamon. Once you find the Oakdale Road–Minnesong Road intersection, it will be the giant potato-shaped twine ball on the left. Call (715) 374–3518 for more information.

IN A BLIZZARD, OF COURSE, YOU COULD ACTUALLY BE DRIVING UP CHRISTMAS TREES
Madeline Island

County Highway H is the official designation of the frozen version of the route between Bayfield and Madeline Island. Automobiles drive across the 2.6-mile stretch of ice, which is outlined with Christmas trees, from January to March. A Run on Water in February promises runners, walkers, and snow-shoers a truly spiritual experience, depending on how you interpret that sort of thing.

When spring approaches and the first car goes through the ice (gradually at first, allowing time to jump out), it's time for

*The Nelson brothers prepare
for another trip along Highway H.*

the Nelson brothers to get out the windsled. It's just the thing
when the ice is too thin for a car but too thick for a boat. The
windsled is a homemade, propeller-driven vehicle that looks
like a small airplane without wings.

Arnie and Ron Nelson offer at least five daily round trips to
commuters, schoolchildren, and shippers of groceries, mail,
library books, and what-all. Their windsled goes 30 to 40 miles
per hour, depending on the ice.

When Highway H melts entirely and becomes Chequamegon
Bay again, cars and passengers return to the services of the
Madeline Island Ferry.

Don't go out there without first calling Arnie or Ron: (715)
747–3300.

WHERE THERE'S SMOKEY
Mercer

Until 1950 Smokey Bear existed only on paper—in posters
and advertisements of the National Forest Service. But that
was before the rangers at the station in Mercer needed an idea
for a parade float for the Fireman's Convention in Hurley in
August. Inspired by a recent Smokey Bear poster, their float
featured a bearskin-and-wood Smokey praying under the sign
AND PLEASE MAKE PEOPLE CAREFUL. AMEN.

Smokey reappeared the following month at the Logging
Congress parade in Wausau, this time in the form of a ranger
wearing a bear costume. Smokey Bear personified was a
big hit!

The idea spread like wildfire, and before long the National
Forest Service was suiting up lots of Smokeys. Today the Wisconsin Department of Natural Resources is officially credited
with fabricating the first Smokey Bear costume.

MOVING IS NEVER EASY

*T*he old-timers had doubts about the wisdom of moving a house across the ice, but the movers (from Minneapolis) said they'd checked it—2 feet thick all the way across. The furnished seven-room, two-story house and trailer (twenty tons) were to be towed from Port Superior to Madeline Island on a truck (ten tons), a distance of slightly more than 3 miles. The ice-wise shook their heads.

On March 2, 1977, the thirty-ton cavalcade set out across the ice. Things went well most of the way but then, just a mile from Madeline Island, the wheels under the house dropped through on one side, and the "Spectacle on Ice" came to a full halt. From the shore the gallery watched the house slowly settle into the water and disappear.

"The only thing sticking up was the chimney of the fireplace," recalls Ed Erickson, a veteran of these waters. "We filled the chimney with sandbags and that didn't go, so then we hauled rock and set rocks on the eaves, and it settled to the bottom of the lake."

In the spring Ed tried to lift the house, but it fell apart. He hauled up the pieces, but the floor is still down there.

The head of the original costume is at the Mercer area Ranger Station. Conservation aide Frank Brunner Jr. created it, and years later forestry technician Dave Sleight rescued it from a warehouse. A good collection of vintage posters is on display too. The Ranger Station is half a mile north of town, on State House Road. Open 8:00 A.M. to 4:30 P.M. Monday and Friday or by appointment. Call (715) 476–2240 for more information.

The nation's first Smokey Bear
head is at the Ranger Station in Mercer.

LARGEST TALKING COW AND CHEESE REPLICA
Neillsville

Chatty Belle is the world's largest talking cow, and the little guy standing next to her—but drop a quarter in the slot and let her tell the story: "Hi, so nice to see you. My name is Chatty Belle and beside me is my son, Bullet. Bullet doesn't talk yet but he's learning. What's your name? [pause] Well, nice to meet you. Did you know I'm the world's largest talking cow? I'm 16 feet high at the shoulders and 20 feet long, seven times as large as the average Holstein." Her voice seems high for such a large cow.

Largest cheese replica, that is.
Cheesemakers ate the real one at their
annual convention.

After reciting statistics of grain consumed and milk produced, Chatty Belle explains about the semi trailer parked next to her. It transported the world's largest piece of cheese, from Wisconsin, of course, to the 1964–1965 New York World's Fair. The rig has glass sides because now it displays the world's largest cheese *replica*, a polystyrene version of the original 14½-by-6½-by-5½-foot cheddar. Now picture 16,000 cows in single file, stretching down the road for 20 miles. *That's* the size of the herd that gave the milk that made the cheese that went to the fair.

Chatty Belle, Bullet, and the cheesemobile face Highway 10 on the east edge of town, next to the Wisconsin pavilion— which, as Chatty Belle explains, represented the state at the World's Fair. It looks like a party hat with an antenna on top.

*W*OOD *T*ICK *C*APITAL OF THE *W*ORLD
Oxbo

Each spring hundreds of people join the ten residents of Oxbo for the annual wood tick race, a strange little insect derby that began in 1979. The race takes place in a tent next to the Oxbo Resort, your basic knotty pine tavern with a couple of heads on the wall and a few cans of Dinty Moore and Sterno on the shelf.

Two contestants at a time take their ticks to the racing table and release them from their little tick carriers (aspirin tins, film canisters, lockets) onto the center of a bull's-eye target. The ticks wander around, and the first tick out of the bull's-eye is the winner of the heat. The mayor of Oxbo smashes the losing tick with a gavel, to ensure that losing-tick genes are not bred again.

WINNING ENTRY IN "WHAD'YA KNOW" 1998 STATE SONG CONTEST

"Wuhdyuh Know About Wisconsin"
by David Slotkoff

Wisconsin is a leader in canning peas.
It invented malted milk and types of cheese.
But it offers much more than these:
Free beer tours, hospitality, festivities.

Wisconsin has low crime rates.
And a larger water-theme park than other states.
Door County has more state parks and shoreline
Than any other county in America so fine.

Elkhart Lake's June Sprints present
The world's largest amateur motor event.
Milwaukee's Summerfest is, y'all,
The nation's largest music festival.

Wisconsin is a leader in canning peas.
It invented malted milk and types of cheese.
But it offers much more than these:
Free beer tours, hospitality, festivities.

The competition continues until only two ticks remain. The one that survives the championship heat wins a cash prize, a trophy, and a place in the Wood Tick Hall of Fame.

"Big Daddy Gulper" won in 1999, eliminating 109 other competitors.

"We have a lot of fun doing something incredibly stupid," says one of the regulars.

The event is held on a Saturday in May. Located just off Highway 70 at the Flambeau River, 15 miles west of Park Falls. Call (715) 762–4786 for details.

WISCONSIN CONCRETE PARK
Phillips

Of all the Wisconsin folks who toted bags of cement for their art, Fred Smith was one of the most prolific. In this Northwoods town he created more than 200 huge figures of animals and people: moose, fish, lions, owls, pioneers, soldiers, angels, kings, and queens. For features and other details he used insulator knobs and pieces of brown beer bottles and bleach bottles and blue Mason jars.

Fred's figures don't just stand there like statues. They're drinking beer, celebrating a double wedding, riding around on horses. The output is amazing for one person, especially considering that Fred didn't get started until age sixty-three. People thought Fred had really gone round the bend when, in about 1950, this fantastical world began to appear in the pine grove next to his Rock Garden Tavern.

Cutting to the chase of the creative urge, Fred confessed, "Nobody knows why I made them. Not even me. The work just came to me naturally."

Fred's place was always a lively gathering spot. The dances and musical events that took place in his barn were legendary, with Fred playing fiddle or mandolin and keeping time with bells strapped to his legs. These days the Friends of Fred Smith hold an annual celebration in August, with puppets or people dressed up like the statues acting out the story of Fred's life.

Concrete Park, open year-round, is located on the southern edge of Phillips on Highway 13. No admission charge but, as Fred used to say, "Donations appreciated." Call (800) 269–4505 for more information.

Fred Smith remembered friends, local
history, and folklore at his Concrete Park in Phillips.

FROM YOUNG SHAVERS
MIGHTY CARVERS GROW
Shell Lake

J oseph Barta (1904–1972) was a high school math teacher
and basketball coach who, for some reason that he could
not explain, had wanted to carve the Last Supper since he was
sixteen. He'd started carving—"whittling," his family called it—
when he was ten.

His family wasn't especially encouraging either. "You'll cut
yourself, Joe," his mother warned. "I'm tired of cleaning up
your mess of shavings," his sister complained. Joe wasn't even
a churchgoer. Yet the compulsion to carve the monumental
piece became almost consuming.

By the time Barta was in his forties, he had left teaching to
carve full time. The Museum of Woodcarving in Shell Lake
shows what can happen when you do that. The collection
includes hundreds of miniatures (prehistoric creatures; every
variety of cow, dog, and woodland creature; JFK on a campaign
swing through Spooner), and life-size re-creations of biblical
figures—not only the 26-foot-long Last Supper (representing
four years of carving) but Christ from nativity to crucifixion,
as well as Daniel in the lions' den. One of the lions looks like
Joseph Stalin; elsewhere, Herod, from the New Testament,
looks like Adolf Eichmann. A coincidence?

The Barta woodcarving collection—the largest created by
one man—was exhibited at the Disney Epcot Center for two
years, but now it is back in northern Wisconsin, where it grew.
The collection is on Highway 63 just north of Shell Lake. Open
daily 9:00 A.M. to 6:00 P.M. from May 1 through October 31.
Call (715) 468–7100 for more details.

WHERE GUYS KEEP SCRATCHING "JFK" ABOVE THE URINAL
Spooner

The Buckhorn Bar on the main street of Spooner is festooned with taxidermy, as are many taverns in the area. But particularly noteworthy here are the two-headed calf and the plaques on the door of the men's room: JOHN F. KENNEDY USED THESE FACILITIES ON MARCH 18, 1960 and GOVERNOR TOMMY G. THOMPSON USED THESE FACILITIES ON MAY 3, 1997.

Senator Kennedy had stopped in to shake hands after a campaign speech outside on the main street of Spooner. He didn't finish the beer someone bought him, but he did use the men's room before returning to the campaign trail. It is not known whether he washed his hands afterward, since he was not an employee.

Grasping the historic significance of these acts under the roof of the Buckhorn that day, the owner enshrined the beer glass in a special case and ordered a plaque for the door. He checked the men's room as well, but saw nothing of museum quality. Thirty-seven years rolled by and, don't you know, Wisconsin Governor Tommy Thompson drops in one day with some fishing buddies, empties a beer glass, and visits the men's room. And—his secretary was named Kennedy. The plaque in his honor appeared not long afterward.

The Buckhorn is on the corner at 105 Walnut, a block east of Highway 53 on the main business street of Spooner. It also has a beautiful wood-and-glass backbar that the Leinenkugel Brewery installed in the 1930s. For more information call (715) 635-6008.

Elvis Aron Presley
owns and operates historic Bloom's Tavern in Phillips. "Everyone
called me Elvis," says the professional Elvis impersonator, "so I decided
to legally change my name." And he did. He also recently ran for mayor
against the incumbent, who prefers heavy metal. Bloom's is located at
396 South Avon Avenue, just a block off Main Street. The tavern is
107 years old and on the National Register of Historic Places.

URBAN AND RURAL WISCONSIN LEGENDS

1. *Cows—how much should you tip? Cow tipping (the pushing over of a sleeping cow by bored adolescent farm youth before they get the keys to the pickup) appears to occur, along with flicking your Bic on cows' methane emissions and putting the odd goose egg under the odd hen. The domino effect—collapsing an entire chorus line of cows—has never been documented. Two good-sized youths working in concert can provide a Holstein with a thrill she'll never forget. One tip: Make sure you rush from the uphill side.*

2. *The Cow with the Porthole. Since we're on the subject, yes, there is a cow with a porthole (several in fact) in the dairy barns at the University of Wisconsin in Madison. The device allows access to the fascinating rumens of the ruminates, which gives animal husbanders something to think about (if cows had as many brains as stomachs, they'd be Einsteins instead of Holsteins). Having actually seen a cow with the window of opportunity, I will tell you that I was somewhat disappointed; it was not like the access on a front-loading dryer, and you couldn't see anything going around inside. By the by, the university is working on genetic designer milks by milking white mice. How do they do it? Tiny little stools.*

3. *Sasquatch summers in Wisconsin. A large (if you consider 7 feet tall large), hairy, manlike creature has been sighted numerous times in northern Wisconsin, although most times it turns out to be a large, hairy man. But not always. In 1992 an oversize hirsute primate with a skunklike odor was spotted alongside a Jefferson County highway, standing over a roadkilled raccoon,* *apparently deciding how to prepare it. The sighting, however, was by two guys from Illinois who simply may not be used to folks up here. (Frankly, we've seen worse in Chicago, and with pinky rings.)*

4. *There are Socialists in the sewers of Milwaukee. Wrong. The Socialists built the sewers of Milwaukee, one of their most fundamental contributions. Milwaukee had many Socialist politicians and mayors, until we discovered they were National Socialists.*

5. *The Virgin Mary has appeared in a bathtub in Kenosha. True—in fact, in many bathtubs, the backyard bathtub grotto being endemic to Kenosha and Racine Counties, where religious and handy Sicilian immigrants, putting in showers during bathroom remodels, stuck the old tubs on end in the backyard with the Virgin standing in them. Some of them are quite elaborate, with masonry, lights, and, yes, running water. Head out Highway 50 and peek into a lot of backyards—my favorite is in Paddock Lake.*

6. *An intact flying saucer landed and is preserved in Appleton, Wisconsin. A case of mistaken identity—that round, futuristic structure with the rotating lights is actually the Aid Association for Lutherans, the place for all your Lutheran insurance needs. Wisconsin has had its share of sightings, abductions, and ignition points on squad cars ruined by interference from alien craft, although most are thought to be from Highland Park, Illinois. Elmwood is building a landing strip and beacon for extraterrestrial craft, so there you go.*

7. *Are those llama herds? Yes, around Eau Claire. They're ornery beasts, though, and would just as soon spit as look at you.*

8. *Official NFL gear in Green Bay includes green-and-gold caskets. Well, maybe not official, but true. Fred Anger-mann of Wisconsin Vault and Casket designed and makes the caskets, which, not being officially sanctioned by the Packers, do not bear the logo, although the over-all effect is unmistakable. Sixty have been sold so far, several have been interred, and others turn up at tail-gate parties at Lambeau Field. It seems only fitting, since your only hope at season tickets is in the next lifetime.*

9. *Wisconsin emits strange radio frequencies. It's true. And a lot of it has to do with the Navy. In fact, the claim for the first radio broadcast of any kind is held by a Navy project. In 1917 station 9XM in Madison broadcast exotic AM waves to ships at sea and held on to become the nation's first public radio station, WHA (by chance, the home of Michael Feldman's Whad'ya Know?).*

Not content with this early success, in the 1980s the Navy constructed a huge and controversial low-fre-quency antenna that is buried in a giant oval beneath thousands of acres of Northern Wisconsin woods. Known alternately as "Project ELF" (for "extremely low frequency") or "Sanguine," it is designed to communicate with submerged nuclear submarines during time of war should everything topside be, shall we say, inoperative. In the event of a third and final world war, the signal to launch will come from us.

10. *Without Wisconsin, there would be no rock-and-roll. Well, without Wisconsin's Les Paul, there would be no rock-and-roll as we know it. Working in his garage in West Allis in 1941, Paul attached a string to a railroad tie and came up with the prototype for the solid-body electric guitar, without which Jimmy Paige, Pete Townsend, Frank Zappa, and Chuck Berry would not have been possible. Les Paul's first working model was, in fact, dubbed "the log," and later metamorphosed into the beautiful Les Paul Gibson. The solid-body electric guitar allowed sustain and distortion, and if you have sustain and distortion, you have rock-and-roll.*

NORTHEAST

THINGS THAT GO SLITHER
IN THE NIGHT
Amherst Junction

Conventional wisdom advises against trying to teach a pig to sing because it can't be done and, besides, it annoys the pig.

Worms seem to be another matter. The worms in Amherst Junction can paint pictures and dance, although someone first has to dip them in paint (nontoxic) and play Hawaiian music (the vibrations turn them on). The most accomplished among them is Herman, a 16-inch Canadian earthworm that has not only danced and painted but learned to play basketball.

At the height of his show biz career, the well-traveled Herman

"I love worms and worms love me," says George Sroda, the Worm Czar of Amherst Junction.

was making the rounds of Hollywood talk shows and doing interviews all over the country. To play basketball he pushed a pea-size basketball across a miniature court and dunked it through a tiny hoop. Painting and dancing came naturally, but teaching Herman to play basketball required quite a large chunk of George Sroda's time.

George is Herman's trainer, agent, biographer, and protector from robins. He has a private research laboratory in Amherst Junction where he takes care of millions of earthworms, which he now is more interested in studying than in exposing to the arts. Today he concentrates on their soil and their diet—high in protein, carbs, minerals, and vitamins—and promotes the joys and rewards of raising earthworms. His book *No Angle Left Unturned: Facts About Nightcrawlers and Red-worms* (now in its eighth printing) has inspired thousands of breeders, gardeners, and fishermen to raise earthworms at home as a hobby or a business. Schoolchildren, retirees—anyone with a few dollars and an old refrigerator can do it. To learn more about worms, write to George at Box 97, Amherst Junction WI 54407, or call (715) 824–3868.

Herman shrank up a bit under the TV lights and retired from show biz some time ago. "To Tell the Truth," "What's My Line," David Letterman, and Johnny Carson are distant memories. You might say he's living on borrowed time, since the lifespan of a Canadian earthworm is about twenty years, but thanks to George's good care Herman has not yet gone to that big peat pile in the sky.

HOUDINI: GOT MILK?
Appleton

Being the son of a rabbi, perhaps Harry Houdini's greatest escape was not going to the yeshiva and finding himself a nice little congregation in Appleton. But Harry could also wriggle out of rolltop desks, piano cases, coffins, and steamer trunks. Even tossing some such thing into the river—with Houdini in it—was not too much to ask of the greatest escape artist who ever lived.

In one famous trick Houdini told the audience to take a deep breath, took one himself, and then disappeared into a sixty-gallon milk can filled with water. Assistants sealed the can shut. On stage a clock ticked away . . . and away . . . and

*Sculptor Richard C. Wolter
signed the lock on* Metamorphosis *"Best wishes, Houdini." It's on a
plaza just south of College Avenue, near the intersection with Appleton Street. A marker nearby notes that Houdini was "a high-spirited
and troublesome little boy who one night unlocked the front-door
locks of all the merchants on College Avenue."*

away. No sign of Houdini. People started to panic and take off, leaving him to reappear to a greatly diminished house.

That very milk can and the rest of the story can be found at the Houdini Historical Center, along with straitjackets, handcuffs (including a pair that President Garfield's assassin wore first), a 1600s-era iron maiden that challengers built for Houdini, and other artifacts related to his life and career.

Houdini spent several idyllic childhood years in Appleton and called it his hometown, although he was born in Hungary. (He died in Detroit of peritonitis, the Tony Curtis movie version of his life notwithstanding.) Houdini's boyhood home and the spot on the Fox River where he nearly drowned are among fifteen locations on a Houdini walking-tour map available at the Historical Center. It explains the presence, elsewhere in Appleton, of the Houdini Lounge, Houdini Elementary School, and Houdini Square.

The Houdini Historical Center is at the Outagamie County Museum, 330 East College Avenue. The museum also has an Edna Ferber exhibit and walking-tour map. The Ferber and Houdini maps both show where Appleton's favorite daughter interviewed its favorite son for the *Crescent* in 1904. Open year-round 10:00 A.M. to 5:00 P.M. Tuesday through Saturday (and Monday from June through August), noon to 5:00 P.M. Sunday. Admission charge. For more information call (920) 733–8445 or visit www.foxvalleyhistory.org/houdini.

Great Lakes Kraut Company of Bear Creek is the world's largest manufacturer of sauerkraut. It produces about 50,000 tons a year and ships much of it to other companies. Its own label is called Krrrisp Kraut.

THE MEASURE OF A MAN
Black Creek

A few miles south of Black Creek, along Highway 47, are
hand-lettered signs that shout not about the Apocalypse,
not about gun control, but about a humble unit of measure-
ment: the inch.

Some years ago, when he worked as a carpenter, James
Franklin Brunette determined that what the United States
Bureau of Standards is trying to pass off as the inch is actually
0.9375 of that amount. (Anyone who has ever bought a two-by-
four would tend to agree.)

If one barley corn is a third of an inch, and a real inch
measures 0.9375, then . . . um . . .

Beyond Brunette's driveway and scattered throughout his property are many exhibits that demonstrate his intriguing proposition. Wheels and contrivances are covered with millions of numbers, painstakingly hand-painted in primary colors to six decimal places, to compare and show the progression of German millimeters, English millimeters, and our joke of a U.S. inch. The most elaborate is his Stonehenge, a huge circle of stones and flags and bags that proves the folly of taking the Bureau of Standards at its word.

Brunette, a.k.a. "Magnifico the Math Master, Arithmetician Extraordinaire," is concerned about the ramifications of it all, for everything from dot-matrix printers to highway safety. He holds forth on the subject at 5107 Highway 47, Black Creek. You can reach him at (920) 739–0733.

IS THAT A GREAT WALL OR WHAT?
Clintonville

Four-wheel-drive technology was developed here early in the twentieth century, and in the 1920s Walter Olen and the company's heavy-duty trucks traveled far and wide. They helped build railways in China, a project that led to Olen's hauling home a hefty souvenir: a portion of the Great Wall of China, which, to date, has protected Clintonville from possible invaders from the North. A gift from revered statesman Sun Yatsen, it is believed to be the only section of the Great Wall ever to leave China.

Eventually Olen's 1,700-year-old Chinese bricks were joined by stones from such places as Jerusalem, the Petrified Forest, Yellowstone National Park, and the Dakota Badlands, along with a Wisconsin millstone. The exotic mementos are lined up in Pioneer Park on the banks of the Pigeon River (where huge flocks of pigeons used to roost in the trees) near two historic houses and the Four Wheel Drive Museum, which displays original four-wheel-drive vehicles—a must visit for SUV or urban assault vehicles seeking to return to their roots. The museum is open from 1:00 to 4:00 P.M. each weekend from Memorial Day to Labor Day.

The Great Wall of China at Clintonville.

THE LOST DAUPHIN

*I*n De Pere's Lost Dauphin Park there was once a humble log cabin that was thought to have housed the rightful pretender to the throne of France, Prince Louis XVII. He was known in these parts as Eleazer Williams. What distinguished Williams from the average Badger claiming royal descent was the fact that he was a French child who had been placed among the Iroquois Indians of New York at about the time of the Dauphin's death/disappearance in the Temple in Paris, where his parents and sister were also imprisoned. If the story was to be believed, the sickly dauphin was smuggled out of Paris by his jailer Simon, and with the help of former servants he was transported to the New World and placed among the St. Regis band in New York.

As a missionary and liaison to the Oneida tribe, Williams emigrated with them to Wisconsin in 1821 and became an influential leader—seeking, some said, to establish an Indian kingdom under his rule. His Bourbon origins were apparently unknown to him until a visit made to Green Bay in 1841 by Prince de Joinville, son of King Louis-Philippe. In one of the stranger evenings at the Astor Hotel, the prince informed Williams that he was indeed the son of Louis XVI and Marie Antoinette, offering him a considerable estate if he would renounce all claims to the French throne.

None of us around here was born yesterday, and Williams was no different: He refused to sign and held out for a better deal. Unfortunately, that never came, and he eventually died penniless in his little cabin in the woods.

While the Reverend Williams never assumed the throne of France, it is a fact that for many years following his death, scores of Oneida children were named Eleazer. Visitors can climb the hillside in the park off County Highway D (Lost Dauphin Road), just north of Little Rapids Road, and take in the Fox River—the beautiful domain of the "Lost Dauphin."

A Spear and a Beer

*W*here can you spear a 200-million-year-old living fossil? At Lake Winnebago, in the heart of Wisconsin's Fox Valley. The prize? Hiawatha's Mishe-Nahma, the "King of Fishes," Acipenser fulvescens, a.k.a. the lake sturgeon. They're supposed to be pretty good eating once you pry off the bony plates and smoke 'em. And although the number of females allowed to be

Bill Casper of Fond du Lac at his fishing shack in fair weather. He spearheaded a movement to protect Lake Winnebago sturgeon by founding Sturgeon for Tomorrow.

taken is strictly controlled, it is not impossible to fork some caviar on a very good day.

 The catch is that, thanks to much-needed conservation limits, the sturgeon season is lightning-short, so the window of opportunity closes quickly. You'll need a spear, some beer, a decoy, a chain saw with an ice bar (you may just want to pay the ten bucks and have a hole cut), a permit, and a shanty painted in Packer colors to park on the ice.

 If you miss your great white, don't worry—sturgeon can live up to 150 years, which should give you more cracks at catching one than you're probably going to need. The upside is, should the Lord send a sturgeon to your hole, it'll be hard to miss, the record on Winnebago being 6 feet 6 inches and 180 pounds—although that may have been a spearer from last season who just surfaced.

 The season opens the second Saturday in February and may close the third, so put down your $10 and take your chances—and don't neglect to be weighed, measured, sexed, and tagged by the waiting DNR biologist, especially if you get a fish. It's not easy—it took one guy from Fond du Lac twenty-three years of drinking Old Style to spear his first sturgeon; hence the saying, "Patience is a sturgeon." If you do get one, they'll hear about it in real time on Jerry Schneider's radio show over WMBE in Chilton.

 Oshkosh or Fond du Lac is a good starting point for your sturgeon hunt to Lake Winnebago or one of the smaller lakes, such as Poygan.

THESE WALLS DO TALK
Fond du Lac

If you're worried about what the walls would in fact say could they talk, you might want to get the map of talking houses and historic places from the Convention and Visitor's Bureau to find out which ones to avoid. The map indicates various locations around the city where you can stop the car and tune your radio to a certain number on the dial (not the same one every time) to hear what the house has to say. If you want to have the entire multimedia experience, you can sidle up and peep in the windows. Currently wired are several historic houses—as well as a lighthouse, a bar, a church, and a fire station—although there's nothing to stop you from pulling up to any residence in town and seeing what you can tune in to.

The bar, J. D. Finnegan's on Main Street, was formerly called Schmidt Sample House, and it was the scene of the famous Carrie Nation hatchet-swinging episode on July 18, 1902, when several hefty men had to wrestle a hatchet away from the tenacious Ms. Nation. Today she would probably be swinging away at the sign announcing that THURSDAY IS "LADIES NIGHT"—ladies drink free tap beer until midnight.

Ms. Nation would, in fact, be beside herself at this decadent downtown intersection of Main and Division. Across the street is a cocktail lounge, in an otherwise respectable hotel that has welcomed such guests as Eleanor Roosevelt, Jack Dempsey, Gene Autry, Wendell Willkie, and John F. Kennedy. On another corner is Dillinger's Dining and Drinking Establishment (Dillinger stopped here for lunch en route to his Northwoods hideout).

Next on the map itinerary, a church tells about a bishop buried inside. Several stops later an impressive nineteenth-century house reminisces about winter days when dozens of neighborhood children gathered in the side yard for skating and tobogganing, and about rainy days when roller skates thundered across the third-floor ballroom. Just a few blocks away, a house recalls the millionaire land developer and his brother who squabbled over property all the way to the Supreme Court. Presumably charity prevails now that the house is a convent.

The tour points out twenty-four historic places, about half of which talk, which may be more than you want to hear from structures of any sort. So, whaddya think—back to Finnegan's?

Free maps are available at the Fond du Lac Convention and Visitors Bureau, 19 West Scott Street (at the far end of North Main Street). The Bureau also has Talking Country Roads cassettes, available for rent or sale, that offer tours of Fond du Lac County. Call (800) 937–9123 for more information.

Ice was one of the principal products of Green Bay from the 1870s to early 1930. Households, breweries, meat packers, and dairies all needed tons of ice to produce, store, and ship their products. Before cutting tools were mechanized, workers used hand saws and horse-drawn ice plows. It was a very dangerous and competitive business.

HOW WOULD YOU LIKE TO BE
A MILLIONAIRE?
Fond du Lac

A cluster of winning lottery tickets purchased along Fond du Lac's Main Street between 1990 and 1995 earned it the name "Miracle Mile," although it's really more like eight blocks (but for this kind of dough, why quibble?). Eight winning tickets sold here during those years totaled almost $160 million. One of them, purchased just four hours before the drawing, left a high school teacher $111 million richer—and with summers off! Three of those eight winning tickets came from Ma and Pa's Grocery Express. In 1997, when the Wisconsin Lottery introduced the new game Daily Pick 4, its very first winning ticket came from there, too. Stratospheric wins have tapered off somewhat, but at the peak of a recent Powerball frenzy, Ma and Pa's sold 20,000 tickets in one day.

Four tickets sold on other streets in Fond du Lac have been good for another $5 million. Fond du Lucre!

WHAT'S GREEN AND GOLD AND
FEELS THE POWER?
Green Bay

As you approach the Green Bay Packer Hall of Fame in Title-town U.S.A., the landscape grows more green-and-gold. Even the lawn ornaments wear Packer shirts in the famous team colors. Across Lombardi Avenue a homeowner paints a

MURAL DECORATION, BROWN COUNTY COURT HOUSE, GREEN BAY, WIS.

When Jean Nicolet arrived in Bay des Puants

("Bay of Bad Odors"), as Green Bay then was known because of its

swamps, he thought that he had found the northwest passage to the Orient.

For his grand entrance he wore a Chinese robe and fired pistols.

new slogan on his fence each season (in 1999–2000: RHODES RAGE DRIVES THE PACK TO ATLANTA). On the opposite corner stands mecca—green-and-gold Lambeau Field.

The intense bond between the Packers and their fans is apparent throughout the museum, the first ever dedicated to a single professional football team. This attachment is embodied by "1998 Fan of the Year" Melvin Knoke of Appleton. According to the tribute in the lobby, Melvin and his wife, Leone, attended nearly all Packer home games for seventy-one years. His declaration in an NFL television commercial that "My name is Mel Knoke and I feel the power!" was heard round the world.

At tailgate parties outside Lambeau Field,
cheeseheads line up to be photographed with Saint Vince
and his guardian angel (John O'Neill and Mary Beth Johnson
of Cross Plains). The money goes to charity.

His stated priorities of "God, my wife, and the Green Bay Packers, in that order" echo those of Vince Lombardi, deeper inside
the museum.

Fans can also see the fiberglass chest protector that Bart
Starr wore (but not the hair dryer that molded it to his body),
splinters that were lodged in Jerry Kramer's intestines for
twelve years, a photo of little Vince Lombardi in a diaper, the
helmet that Ray Nitschke was wearing when a filming tower
fell on him (and Lombardi's tough-love response: "Oh hell, he's
all right"), the shoe that Don Chandler wore for the kick that

led to raising the goal posts, and many other artifacts. You'll find a brick-size package of authentic Frozen Tundra from an undefeated-on-Lambeau-Field season; souvenirs of the 1967 Ice Bowl, when temperatures dropped to minus thirteen; and a great many significant helmets, jerseys, and footballs. The most popular exhibit features authentic replicas of the three Super Bowl trophies in three-quarter size (Packer officials keep an eye on the real ones). Four theaters show film clips of great moments and follies.

The Green Bay Packer Hall of Fame, 855 Lombardi Avenue, is 1.3 miles east of Highway 41 (exit 167). Open daily year-round: 9:00 A.M. to 6:00 P.M. in June, July, and August; 10:00 A.M. to 5:00 P.M. the rest of the year (closed Christmas Day). Admission charge. You can look for more information at www.packerhalloffame.com, or call (920) 499–4281.

Wisconsin leads the nation in paper making, thanks to several major companies in the Fox Valley. Green Bay calls itself the "Toilet Paper Capital of the World," and early examples of toilet tissue and paper towels and napkins can be seen at the Neville Public Museum in Green Bay. Northern Paper, founded in 1901, made all the paper for Sears Roebuck catalogs, and Fort Howard Paper (1920) became the world's largest producer of paper napkins.

TAKE THE PLUNGE
Kohler

John Michael Kohler got into the plumbing business in 1883, when he enameled the inside of a dual-purpose horse trough/hog scalder, attached four legs, and sold it to a farmer as a bathtub. Little did he know what he had set in motion.

Today the bathroom products of Kohler Co. are admired near and far. Kohler Co. has artist-edition sinks that are embellished with moss roses and tell fairy tales ("Once upon a time a youth was enamored of a beautiful girl but a frog cast a spell . . ."), or that depict panoramas of Kohler's award-winning Whistling Straits golf course.

A museum at the Kohler Design Center traces the evolution of plumbing fixtures from hog scalder to the Provincial line, with its country meadow of rabbits, birds, and flowers. Original pieces tell the story—zoned bathrooms of the 1940s and 1950s had separate areas for each activity and triggered the master-bedroom suite; gracious-living bathrooms of the 1980s with whirlpool baths and fine furniture introduced sensory appeal.

Across the street free guided "Industry in Action" factory tours walk visitors through the manufacturing process, from the unbaked gray clay to today's ever-popular white, colored, or embellished toilet, sink, or tub. The three-hour tours begin at 8:30 A.M. Monday through Friday. Call (920) 457–3699 to sign up. The Kohler Design Center, 101 Upper Road, is open 9:00 A.M. to 5:00 P.M. Monday through Friday, 10:00 A.M. to 4:00 P.M. Saturday and Sunday. More information can be found at www.kohlerco.com.

You will never look at your toilet the same way again.

The Great Wall of China at Kohler.

FORTY-SIX-INCH SHOES WITH SPIKES
Lake Tomahawk

For people, unlike myself, who've never had the experience of walking around in 46-inch-long shoes, Lake Tomahawk offers a novel form of sport—baseball on snowshoes. Imagine going for a ground ball with contraptions that measure 12 inches wide and nearly 4 feet long attached to your feet! Imagine sliding into second! The 16-inch ball doesn't necessarily make it easier. The action is ludicrous and exciting.

While other slackers have been out curling, the people of Lake Tomahawk have been playing snowshoe baseball for many years, and are virtually unbeatable. Sometimes they even play in winter, but it's a shorter, seven-inning game with a blaze-

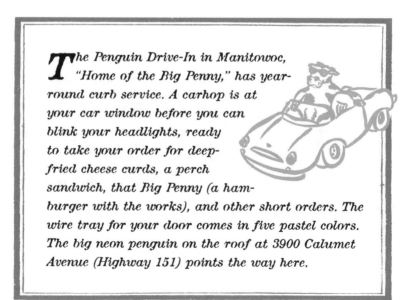

The Penguin Drive-In in Manitowoc, "Home of the Big Penny," has year-round curb service. A carhop is at your car window before you can blink your headlights, ready to take your order for deep-fried cheese curds, a perch sandwich, that Big Penny (a hamburger with the works), and other short orders. The wire tray for your door comes in five pastel colors. The big neon penguin on the roof at 3900 Calumet Avenue (Highway 151) points the way here.

orange ball, given the subzero weather and all that snow. The hope is that someday it will be an Olympic demonstration sport. Wouldn't hurt the Lake Tomahawk economy one bit.

The regular season begins the last Monday in June and ends the second Monday in August (with an extra game on the Fourth of July, before the fireworks). The concession stand opens at 5:00 P.M., and the game starts at 7:30 P.M. Admission is free, and games are held at the Athletic Field, a block west of Highway 47. Call (715) 277–2116.

THE SECRET LIFE OF DENTISTS
Manitowoc

Visitors are flabbergasted when they first enter Rudy Rotter's Museum of Sculpture. His artwork fills an old warehouse that's two stories high and half a block long. Sixteen thousand pieces!

All this from a dentist who was a late starter as an artist, and self-taught to boot. Rotter's dental practice was well under way when he began doing art, creating pieces in his basement studio in between patients or while waiting for the anesthetic to take effect. Upstairs he was a perfectionist; downstairs, an expressionist.

The variety in Rotter's museum is as amazing as the volume: carvings, sculptures, assemblages, drawings. He often uses materials that local industries discard—aluminum, pattern parts, paper. A box of shiny metal from a junkyard led to lasting ties with Dave's Trophy Company. Rudy transforms everything into art with constant themes: man and woman, woman and child, family. Recently the Kohler Foundation purchased 200 pieces for its museum collection.

Rudy is eighty-seven now and working in his studio every day. *"Vissi d'arte,"* sings soul sister Tosca from the CD player.

By creating continuously, he says, new things develop "like variations on themes in music. I'm doing this purely as an amateur in the true sense of the word, for the love of doing it."

Rudy Rotter's Museum of Sculpture, 701 Buffalo Street, Manitowoc. It's best to call first: (920) 682–6671.

For the pieces on the wall,
self-taught artist Rudy Rotter used teakwood
left over from the multimillion-dollar yachts that a
former dental patient builds.

THE FAMILY THAT STILT WALKS TOGETHER . . .
Marshfield

Travis Wolf holds a Guinness World Record for walking on stilts. On March 10, 1998, he took twenty-six steps on stilts that measured 40 feet 10¼ inches from the ground to his ankles. He was sixteen years old at the time and broke the record set by his father, "Steady Eddy" Wolf, in 1988.

Travis climbed a scaffold (usually he rides up in the bucket of a crane) to the top of the stilts, then eased into the stilts and walked those twenty-six steps without touching his handrail wires. The event took place outdoors at Universal Studios in Orlando. Such concerns as wind and a big audience hadn't been present when he was practicing in the silo back in Wisconsin, but all went well.

His younger brothers and sister—Tony, Jordan, and Ashley—also stilt walk, and Travis and Tony appear as the "Sky High Guys" at special events around the country. Mother is the only one who would rather stay on the ground, perhaps because she prefers skirts. Or it may be a guy thing.

JURUSTIC PARK
Marshfield

Long ago, during the Iron Age, creatures inhabited the McMillan Marsh north of Marshfield. After many centuries they became extinct. Some succumbed to corrosion from acid rain. Others were harvested for body parts. Farmers used turtle shells for drinking cups, bird carcasses for shovels, and legs for bicycle forks. . . .

The mighty Marsh Dragon

makes an appearance at the Mitchel Conservatory in Milwaukee.

Fortunately, enough body parts survived intact that most creatures could be reconstructed. We can see them today: the Whirlysaurus, the largest known airborne marsh creature; the Bong Bird, whose wing feathers supply the Fiskars plant in Spencer with blades for grass clippers; the Marsh King, which dressed in drag and ruled the marsh; the Positron, whose head bobs in agreement; the Marsh Mouse, which leveled enemies with methane gas; the Feathered Turtle, slow to get off the ground but once up, up there for months; Dorks.

These huge and complex rusted-metal creatures and their history spring from the wide-ranging imagination of Clyde Wynia, a retired attorney. Where does he get his ideas? "I just keep digging in the marsh." How long does it take to make one? He says he doesn't know and doesn't care. "All I want to do is play."

To get there from Highway 97, go about 3½ miles north on Highway E, then west on U-shaped Sugar Bush Lane.

DEATH'S DOOR

*I*t's hard to believe that Wisconsin's Nantucket, beautiful Door County, gets its name from *Porte des Morts*—"Death's Door," the treacherous passage between Green Bay and Lake Michigan that has claimed thousands of vessels and hundreds of lives over the years.

The most famous of these wrecks may have been the explorer La Salle's hide-laden schooner the Griffin, which disappeared in high seas in 1680. The legend of a seemingly impassable strait goes back at least to the ongoing wars between the Winnebago and Potawatomi tribes, which stretched across the passage between the northern tip of the peninsula and Washington Island. A fire beacon set by the Winnebagoes to lead a Potawatomi war party toward the rocky shoals caused a flotilla of canoes to be dashed against the rocks. Hundreds of warriors were killed, and their bodies continued to wash up on nearby Detroit Island for years. In 1871 a hundred vessels were reported lost in "The Door." And in 1913, during the "great blow" when hurricane-force gales lashed the Great Lakes for three November days, twenty ships with 248 men went down. Today, even with sophisticated navigational aids and charts, only the most experienced of sailors attempt the *Porte des Morts*.

The Door County Maritime Museum in Gills Rock, at 12724 Wisconsin Bay Road, is a good place to learn more about the history of "The Door." And if you would like to sail, boat, or arrange for a charter, the chamber of commerce Web site (doorcountyvacations. com) can point you in the right direction.

SOME, SEEING A HOLE,
LEAVE IT AT THAT
Montello

Mother Nature gave Montello lakes, rivers, and babbling brooks. Irving Daggett gave Montello four waterfalls, one of them 40 feet high, right in the center of town. The waterfall site was once a working granite quarry, Montello's leading industry for almost a century. The end of quarrying in 1976

Where once the ground shook at blasting time,
a little musical church plays recorded hymns, and swans glide
across the old granite quarry at Montello.

left Montello with an enormous hole in the ground, but Daggett, a local realtor and Christmas-tree farmer, saw possibilities there.

He bought the quarry and paid for the construction of the four falls that tumble year-round into the quarry, which now is filled with spring water to depths of 100 feet. He also added a miniature church that rings with religious or patriotic carillon music at various times throughout the day and, in a quarry alcove at Christmastime, a life-size nativity scene. The quarry property occupies about ten acres along Montello Street (Highway 23) between Daggett Realty and Kwik Trip, and incorporates a fifth waterfall, which the Lions Club built back in 1969.

Two other imposing sights lie just west of downtown on Highway 23 near the Marquette County Courthouse. One is the largest tree in Wisconsin, a giant cottonwood. The last time it was measured, in 1978, it was 138 feet high and 23 feet around. The other is Le Maison Granit, an awesome, plum-colored mansion built in 1909 of, yes! Montello granite!

Granite from the quarry at Montello won a gold medal at the 1893 World's Fair as "100% harder than any other granite." Purplish-red in color, it was chosen from more than 280 other granite samples in 1897 as the monument stone for Ulysses S. Grant's tomb.

KISSINGER: MORE THAN A LADY KILLER

*I*t was Henry Kissinger's lucky day when Meldon Maguire came along. Meldon has a dairy farm near Mosinee and serves on the Board of Supervisors.

Late one night in September 1997, along Highway 153 about 9 miles west of Mosinee, Meldon was heading home from a supervisors' meeting and saw flashing taillights up ahead. He stopped his truck at the scene and put on his red "First Responders" vest. (First Responders respond to emergencies and offer assistance.)

Meldon got out and saw guys in suits standing around a big limousine with the windshield all bashed in. The limo had hit a deer. Everybody was okay, and the suits asked Meldon for a ride to their hotel. Meldon cleared out the wrappers and pop cans ("Hey, I got three kids"), everyone piled into the truck, and off they went.

Someone said, "This is Dr. Henry Kissinger," but the name didn't ring a bell. "I knew he had something to do with Nixon," said Meldon, "but I was only about five at that time. I almost asked him what he did for a living. Thank God I didn't."

The next day Meldon received a special invitation to join Kissinger and his entourage, as well as former President Gerald Ford, at the renowned Marshfield Clinic, where an addition was being dedicated to another local boy, Melvin Laird, U.S. secretary of defense in the Nixon cabinet (1969–1973).

It was a very full week for Meldon Maguire. He and his wife, Karen, had had a new baby just four days earlier and named her Fawne—before the Kissinger limo–deer accident.

IN MADISON WE CALL THEM PERSONHOLE COVERS
Neenah

No matter how far Badgers may roam, home won't seem quite so far away if they remember to pause at the curb or crosswalk. There they can likely gaze down upon the words NEENAH FOUNDRY CO. NEENAH, WIS.

Most drainage grates and manhole covers bear those words because Neenah Foundry has been meeting the stormwater-management needs of the world for the past century—not only

Even as you sleep, Neenah Foundry is serving you.

manhole covers and drainage gates but also catch-basin covers; gutter inlets; bridge, subway, and building drains; trench covers; valves and gates; and tree grates. If it's manmade and drains into the earth, Neenah Foundry is there.

The company began making plowshares in 1872 and later expanded the product line to include barn-door rollers, sleigh shoes, bean pots, and other cast-iron items. It cast its first manhole covers and sewer grates in 1904. If you're lucky enough, you can even get a souvenir manhole cover with your name on it, like the one that today graces the hearth of Casa Feldman.

BREAKFAST WITH BOZO
New Holstein

A ho-hum-looking building with a name like "The Diner" does not prepare strangers for the sight they behold when they step in the door. Clowns, clowns, and more clowns. Hundreds of clowns. Clown dolls, clown posters, clown lights, clown ornaments, clown cookie jars. With orange hair, red noses, and loud clothes, they frame the windows and doors, hang from the ceiling, lounge against the caketainers.

Reactions range from smiles to hilarity. For some people the effect is temporary; for others it's lifelong. One documented case concerns a man who still dissolves when he recalls his Twilight Zone experience of stumbling upon "the diner with the clowns" one dark and stormy night some years ago.

The owner, in addition to collecting clowns, participates in parades and benefits as an Irish clown in a green costume. The Diner serves breakfasts and meat-and-potatoes lunches in a classic setting of banquettes and U-shaped counters. It's located at 1701 Wisconsin Avenue (Highway 57) in downtown New Holstein. Hours are 6:00 A.M. to 1:00 P.M. Monday through Friday. You can call "The Diner" at (920) 898–4303.

MOURNING BECOMES DuWAYNE

I *don't know about you, but there are mornings when I*
wake up and would like nothing more than to blast a
bird of peace, particularly if one's been cooing outside my
window since six. Well, I may soon have my chance if propo-
nents of mourning-dove hunting in Wisconsin have their way.
And if the feelings of the 27,000 or so people who turned out
for a Natural Resources Board meeting (which usually
draws as many as 37)—22,000 of whom voted to shoot the
Official State Bird of Peace—are any gauge (no pun
intended), they very well may.

DuWayne Johnsrud, a state legislator from Eastman,
has led the charge against the admittedly not very hard to
take dove (whose mourning, after all, does have a "u" in it).
He has even gone so far as to fricassee a mess of them in his
capitol office (don't know where he got them, but there were
noticeably fewer pigeons on the porticos that week) and offer
tiny little drumsticks to all takers to make his point. Taste-
wise, they are said to run somewhat to the crow side of
squab; but as the French say, the sauce is everything. John-
srud notes, "There are those people out there who don't want
you to eat anything that's got a face on it."

If the board approves the hunt, the mourning-dove sea-
son will commence in September 2001 and run annually
through late October, with a limit of fifteen things with faces
on them per day. The downside is that at one time, Wiscon-
sin had the largest nestings of the now extinct passenger
pigeon, which in 1871 packed some 850 square miles at one
sitting—an estimated 136 million birds. The last was shot by
a conservationist in 1899, making the woods safe, once
again, for acorns.

If this sort of thing interests you, contact the Depart-
ment of Natural Resources as to the status of the mourning
dove, and other things with faces that you can hunt in
Wisconsin. Call (608) 266–2621 or visit the Web site at
www.dnr.state.wi.us.

N URSE R ATCHED , Y OU ' RE F IRED !
O s h k o s h

Northern State Hospital for the Insane admitted its first
patient on April 21, 1873. Many improvements have been
made since that day, including a change of name to Winnebago
Mental Health Institute (WMHI). Today this modern psychiatric
facility treats about 300 children and adults of all ages in its
specialized programs.

A museum on the grounds tells about past practices,
patients, and personnel. On the first floor, exhibits display each
of the twenty-six spoons that one patient swallowed, as well as
an impressive variety of items consumed by others—buttons,
leather straps, a bedspring, scissors, checkers, a rubber heel,
a fingernail file, a toothbrush handle, a thermometer, a crochet
hook, tacks, wire, pieces of slate, and coal. A color photograph
that apparently was taken during surgery shows where several dollars' worth of change ended up. Another exhibit indicates the ingenuity of restless patients in making "keys for
elopement"—escape, that is—and weapons.

Upstairs are five more rooms of exhibits. They include uniforms that staff members formerly wore (today they usually
wear street clothes), an electroshock-therapy machine, medical
instruments in cabinets, mannequins in treatment, a wicker
body basket, and laboratory equipment. Photographs and an
audiocassette offer further details from the past, such as statistics on lobotomies. The entire presentation helps visitors appreciate the progress that has been made over the past 125 years
in treating troubled individuals along the shores of Asylum
Bay on Lake Winnebago.

The Juliane Farrow Museum, at 4150 Sherman, is housed
in what formerly was the superintendent's residence; it

includes many original furnishings. The museum is located in the northwest part of the 250-acre grounds that WMHI shares with Wisconsin Resource Center (for about 500 corrections inmates with mental health problems) and the Drug and Alcohol Correctional Center (population about 200). It is located a few miles north of Oshkosh.

From exit 120 eastbound (Highway 110/Algoma Boulevard) of Highway 41, immediately take the first left turn (Snell Road) and follow Snell for about 4 miles. It leads directly to the grounds. The museum is open from 1:00 to 3:30 P.M. on Thursday only, from February through October. For more information call (920) 235–4910, extension 2345.

A well-coifed mannequin models a straitjacket, a relic of the Northern State Hospital for the Insane, now Winnebago Mental Health Institute.

YOU WENT A LONG WAY, BABY DOE

*H*er eyes were blue—bluer than Lake Winnebago—her
ankles were strong, and her hemline revealed more of
her lower extremities (it wasn't nice to say "legs") than the
Oshkosh of 1877 was accustomed to seeing. The only
female entrant in the figure-skating contest, Elizabeth
Bonduel McCourt won first place, the box of chocolates,
and the heart of a handsome spectator, Harvey Doe.

The couple married and moved to the mining town of
Central City, Colorado, where Harvey proceeded to run his
share of the Doe family fortune into a shoestring. The
mine shut down, and so did the marriage ("You have of
corse herd of my sad sad loss in loosing my darling Babe
I am heart broken about it I shal go crazey," sniveled Harvey in a letter home to the folks in Oshkosh). But new possibilities opened up for Elizabeth, or "Baby." (She acquired
the nickname in the rowdy mining towns, as in "There goes
a beautiful —.")

In time Baby's picture was appearing on saloon beer
trays and calendars, and at Leadville she met Horace
Tabor, whose silver mines had made him
one of the wealthiest men in the West
and, by appointment, a United States
senator. His plain and plucky wife,
Augusta, could not compete.

In 1883 Horace and Baby celebrated
their wedding at the Willard Hotel in
Washington, D.C. (Baby
stopped off in Oshkosh to

model her silks and furs for the town gossips). President Chester Arthur, distinguished guests, and a contingent from Oshkosh attended. Baby's gift from Horace was a $75,000 necklace of jewels that Queen Isabella had hocked so that Columbus could discover America. Later they had two daughters, Elizabeth Bonduel Lillie Tabor and Rosemary Echo Silver Dollar Honeymoon Tabor ("Silver Dollar" for short).

Does Oshkosh have a statue, a plaza, or even a bench at the skating rink in memory of the "Silver Queen," the most fabulous woman to emerge from its pioneer era—this Marla Maples, this Monica of the Middle West? It does not, and the Colorado Historical Society has all of Baby Doe's memorabilia, leaving not so much as a maribou feather from her $7,000 wedding gown for the folks back in Wisconsin. But in 1972 the University of Wisconsin–Oshkosh produced The Ballad of Baby Doe, *the 1956 opera by Douglas Moore that had its New York City Opera premiere in 1958 and by now is recognized as the quintessential American opera. It's got politics! the Wild West!! the American dream!!!*

The Ballad of Baby Doe *tells the whole story, right down to the day in 1935 that Baby Doe was found dead—frozen with two weeks' stiffness into the shape of a cross—in a shack outside Horace's Matchless Mine. Horace had gone bankrupt years earlier when the country abandoned the silver standard. "Hang on to the Matchless. It will make millions again," were his dying words in 1899. And that is what Baby Doe did, though it meant shuffling around town with gunnysacks on her feet for shoes in her last years, and finally dying in rags.*

45 x 90 CLUB
Poniatowski

About 5,000 people from all over the world have driven a
maze of county roads in search of a certain 1885 white
frame building with a Blatz sign out front.

It's Gesicki's Bar, the home of the 45 x 90 Club, and behind
the bar is the membership book that everyone came to sign. It
attests that they have stood in the exact center of the northern
half of the western hemisphere—45 degrees north latitude and
90 degrees west longitude, or halfway between the North Pole
and the equator, and halfway between the Greenwich meridian
and the International Date Line. Of the other three spots like it
on the globe, two are under water; the third is in the middle
of China.

John Gesicki instigated the official recognition and landmark. He had a little park outside of town all ready when the
U.S. Geological Survey came to plant the marker in 1969. He
started the club. These days Loretta, John's widow, offers the
book and the pen. She also might put on a tape of Peter and
Lou Berryman singing:

Exactly half the way from the Equator to the Pole
A quarter of the way around the planet as a whole
It's very hard to find it on a map o' county roads
Ridiculously easy on a four-inch globe

Magellan's men said Captain have we gotten very far
We're writing to our mothers just to tell 'em where we are
The Captain said our longitude is fifty on the dot
I don't know where we are but I can tell you where we're not.

A quarter of the way from top to bottom of our earth
A quarter of the way around the planet of our birth
Speaking cartographically it's not extreme to say
It's the most important 'towski in the USA.

What is on the tip of every schoolkid's tongue
What I mean of course besides a wad of gum
The name of a location every grownup knows
Of a church, a couple taverns, and a school that's closed.

I asked an old cartographer where he would rather be
He mumbled there's a place that's always fascinated me
I'll prob'ly mispronounce it he admitted with a sigh
It's P-O-N-I-A-T-O "duBULLYU" s-k-i.
Poniatowski . . .

Poniatowski is about 12 miles west of Wausau and does not
appear on all maps. (The very large Catholic church across the
street from Gesicki's and one or two other buildings comprise
Poniatowski.) From Highway 97 go east on County M and
watch for the left on County U. Gesicki's is closed on Sunday
and Monday. Call (715) 352–3094 for information.

The
first disposable paper
handkerchiefs were produced in
1924 by Kimberly-Clark Co. of Neenah
under the name Celluwipes. Later
they were renamed Kleenex-
Kerchiefs.

A cure for cabin fever in 1939,
smelt wrestling at the Smelt Carnival in Marinette.

ODD BEDFELLOWS
Ripon

Ripon has the distinction of being the birthplace of both the Republican Party and the Wisconsin Phalanx, a distinctly Badger take on Communism in which stock was sold, real estate purchased, and communal adherents rewarded according to their usefulness.

The Socialist band was organized in Kenosha and led in the spring of 1844 to the Ceresco Valley (named for Ceres, the goddess of grain) near Ripon by Warren Chase, a follower of Fourier. The group planted grain, built a grist mill, carpenter shop, school, and the long house (which still stands today). Although it was ideal, it was not free. Board was 63 cents a week (on the other hand, wages averaged out to 7½ cents an hour, and the cost of feeding and clothing the entire extended family was deducted). And while it promoted equality, some were more equal than others in their skills—which, in time, caused some resentment by the less useful.

Still, Utopia does not mean "nowhere" for nothing. Ceresco was a success until a life without "rum, vulgarity, and profanity" seemed to wear on some, particularly after free-love devotees moved in. Others, tired of communal life, set up their own households. But at its height, 200 Communists lived in rural Ripon, some of whom, idealists still, stayed on after the community was sold off in 1850 to join in the formation of the Republican Party, the flower of the strong Wisconsin antislavery movement.

The one-room schoolhouse where this meeting took place on March 20, 1854, is now a historic site at 303 Blackburn Street, about a block off Ripon's main street. The long house is at 26–34 Warren Street.

PRAISE THE LORD AND
PASS THE MORTAR
Rudolph

The Grotto Gardens and Wonder Cave represent the lifelong labors of parish priest Phillip J. Wagner. This site is all the more remarkable if you know that Wagner started here with a potato field and no mortaring experience. His first attempt at grotto building, in 1928, consisted of stacking up rocks. When he realized he'd also need mortar, he stirred it in a bread pan with a kitchen spoon. He got the hang of it, though, and over the next thirty years, Wagner and an equally dedicated member of the parish transformed the potato field into an extraordinary collection of shrines and grottoes.

The Wonder Cave makes this religious grotto unique among others in Wisconsin. From the outside the Wonder Cave looks like a hill of rocks among trees and plantings. Inside, however, it has not only cave ambience—a passageway that winds up and down and around, water trickling down the walls—but also organ music, statuary, and biblical reminders in the form of little tin sheets with perforated words and images, backlighted with colored bulbs. The cave is entirely above ground (unusual for a cave), and the manmade passageway is a fifth of a mile long.

The Grotto Gardens and Wonder Cave at Rudolph are located on the grounds of St. Philip's Parish, 6957 Grotto Avenue. The Wonder Cave and a gift shop are open daily 10:00 A.M. to 5:00 P.M. Memorial Day through Labor Day. The Gardens are open year-round, no charge; there's a small admission fee for the Wonder Cave. For more information call (715) 435–3120.

A RED-NOSED REINDEER
Rudolph

The Village of Rudolph was named in 1856 for the son of an area pioneer, but today it is identified more with a different luminary. About fifty years ago the postmaster proclaimed this to be the red-nosed reindeer's hometown; he started hand-stamping Christmas mail with a statement to that effect and a drawing of the little fellow. In time the local post office was sending out thousands of specially stamped holiday cards each year. In 1999 Rudolph the community (population 450) hosted a first-day-of-issue ceremony for the U.S. Postal Service's new holiday reindeer stamps.

*The
Town of Pound
dropped a ton when 158 residents went on a community
Slim-Fast diet in 1992. Way more
than a ton—2,869 pounds, to be
exact. Those who dare still weigh
in regularly at the village hall.
Only 17 people have put it
all back on.*

HAMBURGER HALL OF FAME
SEEKS FRIED ONIONS HALL OF FAME
Seymour

Charlie Nagreen of Hortonville was only fifteen years old in 1885 when he arrived in Seymour by ox-drawn wagon to set up his meatball stand at the Outagamie County Fair. When meatballs turned out to be not the ideal finger food (especially since he cooked them in butter), Charlie smooshed the meatball between two slices of bread and called it a hamburger.

For the next sixty-five years, Hamburger Charlie was a fixture at the fair. In 1989 Seymour underlined its place in culinary history by cooking and serving to 13,000 people a 5,520-pound hamburger—the world's largest, as recorded in the *Guinness Book of World Records*. When you come to think of it, it's amazing they had to go that high to get the record.

The Hamburger Hall of Fame displays not only Hamburger Charlie's spatula, his red teapot (for the melted butter), and his guitar, but also hundreds of hamburger collectibles: burger jewelry, games, recordings, clothing, radios, telephones, lamps, and so on. A section of items for sale includes yo-yos, french-fry pens, and even a crocheted hamburger with everything, including little round pickle slices ($9.00).

The Hamburger Hall of Fame, 126 North Main Street (a white brick building with a "Home of the Hamburger" mural on the south side), is open Friday through Monday, Memorial Day through Labor Day. A donation is requested. The annual Burger Fest, with parade, bun run, bun toss, and ketchup slide, is held the first Saturday in August.

The grill that cooked the world's biggest burger. They didn't try to flip it.

In 1999 word arrived from Montana of a 6,000-pound hamburger. Home of the Hamburger, Inc., is graciously hanging back until at least the year 2001 to let the Montanans bask in glory while they may. Then, look out.

FROM PLUMBING, ART
Sheboygan

When visitors enter the washrooms at the John Michael Kohler Arts Center, they usually stay inside for a long time. There's a lot to see.

One of the men's rooms tells the social history of architecture in vivid hand-painted tiles, with such phrases posted over the fixtures as "Celebrating Another Conquest," "Boldness Has Genius," "Aspiring Toward Heaven," and "Defending the Castle." Behind tinted-glass cartouches in a women's room are etched the thoughts of Isadora Duncan, Frida Kahlo, and eight other women. Squeezing a bulb attached to each creates a shower of cosmetic powders and soap shavings behind the glass.

This water-pistol bouquet in delft-style, with hand-painted and -glazed tiles, appears over a urinal at the Kohler Arts Center. The artist was Ann Agee.

The six artist-decorated washrooms are one result of
the unique Arts/Industry residency program funded by
Kohler Co., which encourages artists to explore materials
and equipment at its plumbingware factory. The collaboration
has produced many more works, some of which appear in
one of the galleries. They include a large coffee cup that
flushes, Ken and Barbie andirons, and a Squeaky Fromme
nightlight.

Another gallery exhibits works of self-taught Wisconsin
artists. Among them are the elaborate chicken- and turkey-
bone towers of the prolific artist Eugene Von Bruenchenhein,
a Milwaukee baker who so adored his wife, Marie, that he
fashioned elegant crowns of ordinary materials for her. They
are here, as well as the paintbrushes he made from plastic
straws and Marie's hair.

There are surprises elsewhere, too, such as the life-size
ceramic horse by Deborah Butterfield in the formal dining
room of the Kohler family mansion, which stands at the corner
of the recently expanded Arts Center.

The John Michael Kohler Arts Center, 608 New York
Avenue, opens at 10:00 A.M. daily, year-round. (Be there when
the doors open and you probably can safely tour all six washrooms. At other times try a stakeout, followed by a knock on
the door.) It closes at 5:00 P.M. Monday, Wednesday, and Friday;
at 8:00 P.M. Tuesday and Thursday; and at 4:00 P.M. Saturday
and Sunday.

To get here take exit I-43 (exit 126) onto Highway 23 East,
which becomes Kohler Memorial Drive and then Erie Avenue.
Continue east to Sixth Street, turn right, and follow Sixth
Street 4 blocks south to New York Avenue. The entrance to the
Arts Center is on New York Avenue between Sixth and Seventh
Streets. Call (920) 458–6144 for more information, or visit
www.jmkac.org.

THE WRECK OF THE LOTTIE COOPER
Sheboygan

The *Lottie Cooper* was a three-masted schooner that foundered in a howling northeast gale on the night of April 9, 1894. It went down in the Sheboygan harbor and lay there for the next century. Recently her remains were discovered on the harbor floor, during surveying work for construction of a marina. The remains were recovered from the murky floor, reassembled in their original positions, and are now on display on the grounds of the marina.

Divers report greatly improved visibility when a shipwreck, like the Lottie Cooper *in Sheboygan, is on land.*

WINTER FUN IN THE MITTEN-SHAPED STATE

*W*hat's to do when Super Bowl Sunday is over and it's only February? Is life still worth living?

In Sheboygan Falls they race wooden snakes down a hill and cheer them over the finish line. "C'mon, Specklebelly!" "Go, Wise Asp!" They call it the World Champion Snowsnake Races and award trophies to the winners. It takes place the first Sunday in February at Smerke's Sportsmen's Club, on County Highway J about half a mile west of Highway 32. You can find out more at (920) 458–2949.

That same weekend, at Schnee Days in Elkhart Lake, they gather in the snow to bowl downhill and play golf. Call (877) 355–4278 for more information.

An estimated 10,000 ships have been lost on the Great Lakes—700 in Lake Michigan, 60 off Sheboygan, and about a dozen right in the harbor. (Some were hauled up, pumped out, and put back in service, only to sink two or three more times.) *Lottie* represents them all because she's the only recovered shipwreck on display on the Great Lakes today. Text and drawings tell more about her saga.

There are self-tours here as well as guided tours for groups. Call (920) 458–2974 for information.

AND SWEDISH MEATBALLS
UNDER THE ROOF
Sister Bay

Regardless of whether or not Scandinavian houses still have sod roofs, Al Johnson thought a sod roof would be a nice touch for the Swedish restaurant he opened in 1948. The eatery was housed in a log building that was shipped in pieces from Norway to Sister Bay. A friend donated a goat to complete the picture, and after that Al didn't have to worry about advertising. The word spread, crowds gathered, and they still do.

It's best to arrive in some conventional manner, such as by car or on foot. When curious people from Marinette landed their helicopter on the lawn just north of the restaurant one day, the terrified goat leaped off the roof, hurdled a parked car, dodged through traffic, jumped into the bay, and started swimming. Al had to chase after it in a boat for the rescue.

Today more than one goat munches away up there, while diners below select from a more interesting menu, starting with Swedish pancakes with lingonberries for breakfast. Al Johnson's Swedish Restaurant is open 6:00 A.M. to 9:00 P.M. daily. It's located on Bayshore Drive (Highway 42). Call (920) 854–2626 for information.

TONY'S FAN FAIR
Stevens Point

One day in the 1940s, while Anton Flatoff was working at the Whiting Hotel downtown, he saw an old exhaust fan in the trash. Whoever was remodeling the hotel kitchen didn't have Tony's imagination. He took it home; this was the first of many exhaust fans to catch his eye over the years.

Tony's Fan Fair started with

an old exhaust fan from the hotel downtown.

Tony eventually painted the fans red, white, and blue, added some wheels and cool industrial shapes, and assembled in his backyard what he calls "Tony's Fan Fair." It's 12 or 15 feet tall, and when the wind blows, the fans spin and make a soft rattley sound.

On the west edge of Stevens Point, after the intersection of westbound Highway 10 and County Highway C, look to the right from Highway 10 toward the first house on Harding Avenue. Or pull up at 556 Harding for a closer look. Even the shutters on Tony's house are decorated with little fan blades.

THAT'S USING YOUR CHEESE

In November 1995 Frank Emmert Jr., a die-hard Green Bay Packer fan, was flying home to Superior from a Packers–Browns game in Cleveland. As he neared Stevens Point, ice caused his single-engine plane to lose power. Just before impact Emmert grabbed the foam-rubber cheesehead he'd worn at the game and buried his face in it. He believes it saved his face and arms from serious injury (though not his ankle), and maybe even his life.

National wire services picked up the story, and before long Emmert was being wheeled onto the set of The Tonight Show *in a cart that resembled a cheese wedge to tell the story to Jay Leno. Today he still travels with his cheesehead.*

TOOTIE LOVES CHUCK
Two Rivers

Two Rivers is the birthplace of both the ice-cream sundae and Charlton Heston's wife. A re-creation of the soda fountain where Edward Berner first poured chocolate sauce over ice cream in 1881 is among the exhibits at the old Washington House hotel. Less well known but popular for many years, according to a news story posted here, was a five-cent float consisting of a tall glass of milk, a scoop of ice cream, and crushed oyster crackers.

In the Sons and Daughters Room is an exhibit devoted to Lydia Clarke Heston, who is not only Charlton's wife but also the great-great-granddaughter of Hezekiah Huntington Smith, a founder of Two Rivers. Lydia is pictured in her own acting days and with other swimmers in the Polliwog Club of Washington High School. Her annual Christmas letters to a long-time friend are here too. A recent one reports that Chuck is deeply involved in his work as president of the National Rifle Association, that their son-in-law Carlton is working hard for Sotheby's and went to Bali to relax, and that she herself had a photography show at a gallery in Orange County, California. Signed "Tootie and Chuck," several years' worth of newsy letters, each four or five typewritten pages long, are on display with other scrapbook items.

The second floor of Washington House is something like a Wisconsin Sistine Chapel. The walls and ceiling are covered with generic pastoral and patriotic scenes that were created by mural artists in 1906 and restored by a conservator in the 1990s. Originally the room was used for dances, plays, and wrestling matches; today it's the site of concerts, lectures, and other community events.

Washington House is 1 block east of the main street in Two Rivers ("T'rivers" as the natives call it) at Seventeenth and Jefferson Streets, across from a large museum of wood type, and down the street from a history museum that used to be a convent. Open daily year-round from 9:00 A.M. to 9:00 P.M. May through October; 9:00 A.M. to 5:00 P.M. November through April. Call (920) 793–2490 for more information.

LITTLE ICELAND

Washington Island is the oldest Icelandic community in the United States, which is one reason that old iconoclast Thorstein Veblen spent summers there from 1908 to 1926, studying and writing and brushing up on his Icelandic. He'd got The Theory of the Leisure Class *out of his system by that time, but more writing along those lines followed in the secluded cabin he built for himself. Every morning he rowed across Little Lake to chitchat in Icelandic with the Bjarnarssons and pick up fresh milk and butter.*

Door County is the thumb of the
mitten-shaped state of Wisconsin, and Hollis Bridenhagen
was its dedicated sheriff for many years. Today a large limestone
thumb marks Sheriff Bridenhagen's grave in Blossomburg Cemetery
at Peninsula State Park.

POSSIBLY A COW
JUMPING OVER THE MOON?

Most alien craft streaking through Wisconsin are shiny, lighted, wedge-shaped BMWs from Chicago's North Shore, hurtling their crews toward their holiday cabins, but our state is no stranger to craft from somewhere far, far beyond Illinois. In fact, one of the first recorded UFO sightings in America was reported in Eagle on April 14, 1897. A craft "looking like a toy balloon" with red and blue lights hovered near the northern horizon—much amazing Otto Lantz, Dr. Colter, and Will Raiche—before flying on to perplex other communities, including Oconto, Marinette, Darlington, Marshfield, Eau Claire, Kenosha, Madison, Rio, Ripon, and Baraboo (where some skeptics thought it may have had a home base in the Ringling Brothers cosmos).

Dundee Mountain, near the town of Osceola, is a favorite gathering place for those who have seen long, glowing, cigar-shaped or red, triangular hovering objects. They come here hoping for another glimpse—or, in some cases, another proctoscopic examination. Bob Kuehn of Fond du Lac, who attends every year, has seen sixty-five UFOs over the years, the first being a flying washtub when he was four. Bill Benson, the owner of Benson's Hide-A-Way on Long Lake at Dundee and the man behind UFO Daze, an annual summertime event, believes there have been so many sightings in what he considers Wisconsin's Area 51 (of Roswell, New Mexico, fame) because of either our latitude or longitude. Or perhaps it's for the same reason that the beer makers came: "We also have a lot of good water here." Sightings have occurred regularly in Long Lake since an alien craft followed a farmer plowing in 1948.

Jay Rath, in his book The W-Files, cites a Vilas County report of local Joe Simonton's close encounter with a flying saucer "brighter than chrome." It landed in his backyard, disgorging three aliens who served him pancakes that "tasted like cardboard" (which many believe had to be Norwegians bearing lefse). Rath lists several hundred other reported sightings around the state—which, in toto, have got to add up to more than just cabin fever. Belleville and Elmwood (you know, where they planned the UFO landing strip?) both have UFO days, and Bill Benson can fill you in on the latest around Long Lake. The number to call is (920) 533–8219.

NELSEN'S BITTERS CLUB
Washington Island

Bartenders everywhere keep a small bottle of bitters on hand for flavoring drinks—Manhattans usually, and then they use only a dash. But Nelsen's orders bitters by the case, having been a world leader in its consumption ever since the days of Prohibition.

It was then that resourceful Tom Nelsen, who had worked in a bitters factory in Europe before coming to Washington Island, licensed his tavern as a drugstore, upon discovering that bitters was classified as a medicine. (A Prussian surgeon and veteran of the Battle of Waterloo had concocted it for the upset stomachs of Simon Bolivar's freedom fighters in Venezuela.) At 44.7 percent alcohol, the equivalent of 90-proof whiskey, bitters became a popular remedy on the island, although for what is still subject to some debate.

In time the extraordinary consumption of bitters prompted a letter of inquiry from the House of Angostura of Trinidad and Tobago ("By Appointment to Her Majesty") to its very best customer—Nelsen's stocks only the Angostura label—and was surprised to learn that residents of a tiny island were drinking it straight. They still do.

The exact content of Angostura bitters is a deep dark secret, but it's a distillation of various tropical herbs, barks, and roots. Tom Nelsen drank a pint a day and lived to almost ninety, a good enough reason for islanders still to drop in for "a tapper and a shot of bitters."

In the 1950s Tom's nephew Gunnar started the Bitters Club, which is still going strong. Last summer more than 3,000 members were initiated by tossing down a one-ounce shot of bitters and signing the book. Nelsen's Hall Bitters Pub and

Restaurant, open year-round, is on Main Road, about 1½ miles
north of the ferry dock. It recently celebrated its centennial
and, by foiling the feds during Prohibition, it is the bar with
the longest continuous run in Wisconsin. Call (920) 847–2496
for more information.

WANT TO BUY A BRIDGE?
Waupaca

What with London Bridge finding itself in Arizona, it
should not be surprising that the State of Wisconsin, in
its finite wisdom, is looking for a good home for the soon-to-be-
replaced Phillips Bridge, spanning the Little Wolf River
between New London and Weyauwega.

What a bridge it is—eligible for the National Register of
Historic Places as a first-rate example of the single-span steel
truss bridge, cutting-edge technology from the turn of the last
century rendered obsolete by the advent of concrete-and-steel
girders (which are nice, but lack the elan of the truss). We're
talking value here—160 feet of 24-foot-wide classic bridge, in
great shape for its age—why, you'd easily expect to pay
$100,000 for a bridge of this quality; at $50,000 it would be
a steal.

But are you ready for this? It's yours, absolutely free for
the taking, no strings (albeit some concrete pilings) attached!
The perfect complement for that Japanese carp pond you've
been thinking about in the backyard. But you have to hurry;
there aren't many of these left, several already having been
placed on hiking and snowmobile trails and city parks around
the Midwest. True. You have to maintain the bridge's "historical
integrity," but that's subject to interpretation. It's not like

*Students from
Bonduel won the statewide
Badger Spelling Bee six times in
the 1980s. Out-spelling all other competitors from around the state, they
ultimately triumphed with* corolla, canasta,
nidificate, apolaustic, inferentially, *and*
tectonics. *In 1991 a thirteen-year-old girl
from Clintonville won the National
Spelling Bee in Washington,
with* antipyretic *(anything
that reduces fever).*

they're going to take it back if you hang a few lights on it. And if you have many more rivers to cross, there are two more truss bridges just like it sitting in a Dodge County field off Highway 16 begging for adoption.

Free to a good home—just contact the Wisconsin Department of Transportation, (608) 246–3800, and let them know there's a place in your heart for a steel-truss bridge. Limited financing available.

In the 1930s hotels and restaurants were required to serve at least two-thirds of an ounce each of Wisconsin butter and Wisconsin cheese with every meal that cost twenty-five cents or more.

SOUTHEAST

HONEY (THAT'S WHAT I WANT)
Ashippun

The Honey Museum asks the question that many bees would ask had they the time: Where would we be without bees?

I'm not saying that our lives would be impoverished without them, but besides all the wonderful pollination work they do, they give us Crayolas, moustache wax, lipstick, teat dilators, Ukrainian Easter-egg designs, and the little sheets you bite down on for the dentist, above and beyond honey. The Egyptians put honey in tombs for life in the hereafter, and Henry VIII signed all his official documents with a beeswax seal. And that's just two examples.

That's not all, as you shall learn at the museum at Honey Acres. When a bee finds a food source within 50 meters (54 yards), the bee does the *round dance* in quick short steps and runs in circles as other bees crowd around. When food is found more than 50 meters away, the bee does the *wag-tail dance*, and the more rapid the tail wagging, the more exciting the find. If the food is right on the border between 50 and 50-plus, he does the Watusi.

The statistics are awesome. Honeybees must visit two million flowers to gather enough nectar for one pound of honey. If he thought about it beforehand, he probably wouldn't do it: One bee collects only a tenth of a pound of honey in its entire lifetime, and that goes to the queen. It takes many, many bees flying a total of 25,000 miles to produce one pound of honey—that's equal to once around the world. Let's see sugar say that.

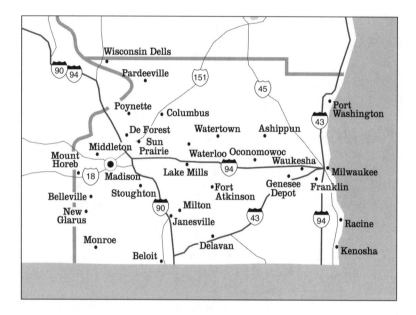

It takes one Diehnelt family five generations of beekeeping to produce one honey of a museum. It is located 12 miles north of I–94 on Highway 67, 2 miles north of Ashippun. Products are for sale in the shop. Free admission to the museum. Open 9:00 A.M. to 3:30 P.M. Monday through Friday year-round; noon to 4:00 P.M. Saturday and Sunday from May 15 through October 30. Call (414) 474–4411 for more information.

TOUCHED BY AN EXHIBIT
Beloit

Many of the host of angels at the Angel Museum are made of porcelain or wood, but some are also constructed from drinking straws, tin-can lids, fur, coal, flower petals, or pasta shells (that's a rigatoni body, bow-tie wings, macaroni arms). The angels sing, fly, nap, leapfrog, sew, knit, sweep, fish, marry, jitterbug, and play musical instruments. They wear not only robes and halos but also raincoats and cheeseheads.

Some function as music boxes, cookie jars, or banks. Some are very small; the second-smallest is an angel-shaped pewter cookie cutter for a dollhouse. There are sets of angels for each day of the week and month of the year. A set of nested angels painted green, pink, and purple is a rarity from Russia. The museum also houses about 600 angels that Oprah Winfrey received after she asked her television audience, "Why are there no black angels?"

The 6,000 pieces in the museum represent only about half of the collection of Lowell and Joyce Berg. It all began one day in 1976 when they went into an antiques store in Florida and came out with two angel figurines. The following Christmas they noticed several angels among their decorations and decided to collect angels as souvenirs when they traveled. Apparently they traveled a lot because after that "it just snow-balled," says Joyce, who usually wears a silver angel costume with wings as she shows visitors around the museum.

From exit 185 on I–90 (at the landmark 40-foot can of chili with beans at the Hormel plant) go west on Highway 81 for about 3 miles, then turn south at the Rock River and look for the red brick church with round windows at 656 Pleasant Street. Open 10:00 A.M. to 5:00 P.M. Monday through Saturday,

May through September; 10:00 A.M. to 4:00 P.M. Tuesday
through Saturday, October through April. 656 Pleasant Street.
Gift shop. Admission charge. For more information call (608)
362–9099 or check out www.angelmuseum.org.

WISCONSIN DISCOVERS COLUMBUS
Columbus

A huge old brick building houses not only Wisconsin's
largest antiques mall but also a museum dedicated to the
city's namesake, Christopher Columbus, who, although he
never visited Wisconsin, would have liked it here. The large collection of Columbus images includes not only plates, busts, and
posters but also many souvenirs from the World's Columbian
Exposition of 1893, which honored his discovery of the New
World some 400 years earlier.

The many depictions of the bearded man in mini-bloomers
against a backdrop of ocean and ships make it easy to guess
what the Exposition's souvenir floaty pens might have looked
like. But plastic was not yet on the horizon, so the souvenirs
instead are substantial and sometimes quaint items made of
metal, paper, and cloth—thimbles, hairpin cases, handkerchiefs, watch-case openers, ice-cream molds, and much more.
An especially impressive non sequitur is a model of the world's
first Ferris wheel, which debuted at the Exposition. It was 250
feet high (nearly as high as the capitol in Madison), and its
brave passengers rode in thirty-six enclosed cars, sixty in each,
for a total of 2,160 people, many more than the *Niña,* the *Pinta,*
and the *Santa Maria* combined.

An exhibit in the quincentenary department tells the story
of a man who drove 30,000 miles photographing every community in the United States that was ever named Columbus, even

THE COW
THAT ROARED

*W*e wuz robbed: Wisconsin is only a shadow of
its former self.

In a lumber swindle instigated by wealthy New
Englanders prior to Wisconsin's admittance to the
Union in 1848, the land between the St. Croix and
the Mississippi Rivers, including some choice
parcels known as Minneapolis and St. Paul, a good
chunk of northern Illinois ranging from Rock Falls
to Chicago, and all of what should be known as the
Upper Peninsula of Wisconsin, were stripped away
from the state. We coulda been a contender, rival-
ing California and New York in electoral votes and
general clout.

The insult to Badger pride was so great that
Wisconsin actually seceded from the union in 1843,
only nobody noticed. Under the dotty James Doty,
territorial governor, Wisconsin declared itself to be
a sovereign and independent (and thereby eligible
for foreign aid) state ready to defend its integrity
and citizenry—in effect, declaring war on the
United States of America. This remains the only
American war in which no skirmishes were fought,
unless it was the one in Congress that caused Doty
to be transferred to Utah, where it was thought he
could do little harm. As in the South, some resentment remains to this day.

if a tree out in the middle of a field was all that was left of it. That is the spirit that settled this great land of ours.

Columbus may be out of favor in many places, but not in Columbus.

Columbus Antiques Mall and Christopher Columbus Museum, 239 Whitney Street, about 2 blocks from the center of the business district. Open 8:30 A.M. to 4:00 P.M. daily. Call (920) 623–1992 for more information.

YOU SCRATCH MY BANK
Columbus

Across the street from a St. Vincent de Paul store and next door to an abandoned bakery stands the Louis Sullivan-designed Farmers and Merchants Union Bank. By the 1920s, when more peas were canned in Columbus, Wisconsin, than anywhere else in the world, the old bank had outlived the telephone building. It was time to build.

Naturally the bank president at first thought along the lines of Greek classical. But for his wife, no ordinary bank would do. She had seen photographs of Sullivan banks and was impressed. The "father of the skyscraper" was summoned, he stayed, he designed.

The play *The Jewel Box* tells the whole story.

The bank is at 159 West James Street. Lobby opens at 9:00 A.M. and closes at 3:00 P.M. Monday through Thursday, at 5:30 Friday, and at 11:00 A.M. Saturday. The mezzanine has a small museum. Call (920) 623–4000 for information.

The jewel box: He thought Greek classical,
she thought Louis Sullivan.

CLONING AROUND AT ABS
De Forest

ABS (American Breeders Service) Global is known to dairy-men worldwide for its leadership in artificial insemination of cattle—and to Wisconsin motorists on I-90/94 for the puns on its billboard at company headquarters (OUR WIT IS A PLAY ON SEMENTICS, explained one).

ABS GENETICS IMPROVE YOUR DAIRY-HEIR. ABS THE CHAMPAGNE OF BOTTLED BULL. ABS IS THE CATTLE-ACT OF THE A.I. INDUSTRY. OUR BEST ASSETS ARE FROZEN. CALL US WHEN YOUR HEIFER'S IN THE MOOED. QUALITY GENETICS—MORE THAN A COWINCIDENT. LET ABS PUT A SMILE ON YOUR COW-TENANTS. MANY ARE CALLED BUT FEW ARE FROZEN. OUR GENES DON'T FADE. WE DELIVER THE MALE. They just keep coming.

ABS Global is also known for producing the world's first cloned calf (named Gene, of course) in 1997, just six months after Scotland announced the clonation of the sheep Dolly (GENETIC PROGRESS IS ALL RELATIVE). By now ABS has a herd of cloned cows.

ABS was founded in 1941, at first employing the delivery technique pictured on page 121, and the company shows signs of staying in business FOR HEIFER AND HEIFER. In 1999 ABS merged with a British company to form the largest artificial-insemination company in the world. WITH ABS MORE PROFIT IS IN THE BAG.

The bullboard is on the east side of I-90/94 between High-way V (exit 126) and Highway 19 (exit 131). For more bovine news, see www.absglobal.com.

County Highway V offers two startling sights. To the west a life-size, flamingo-pink elephant wearing glasses looks down on interstate traffic from the Phillips 66 gas station and mini-mart. To the east a larger-than-life Holstein welcomes visitors to Ehlenbach's Cheese Chalet.

R OMEO AND JULIET
Delavan

Delavan was the home of several circuses, and the elephant that stands on a monument in Watertower Park is a facsimile of a rogue elephant, Romeo, who lived here between 1854 and 1865. One of the largest Indian elephants ever exhibited in America, he stood nearly 11 feet tall and weighed 10,500 pounds. In his day Romeo crushed, tusked, trampled, or otherwise killed five handlers. One time he escaped from his barn and terrorized the area for three days until captured.

An elephant named Juliet was from the same herd, imported from Ceylon (modern-day Sri Lanka) in 1851 for the P.T. Barnum Asiatic Caravan. Juliet was as delightful as Romeo was dangerous. She pulled a bandwagon in street parades, performed in the ring, and generally charmed her trainers.

Because she died in the month of February, in 1864, when the ground was frozen, Juliet's body was weighted down and deposited through a large rectangular hole sawed in the ice of Lake Delavan. In May 1897 a man trolling for northern pike off Lake Lawn reeled in part of a rib cage thought to have belonged to Juliet, and in 1931 a drag-line operation yielded a tibia. Presumably the rest of her bones are still on the bottom of the lake. Romeo died in Chicago in 1892 after surgery for a foot infection, but the month was June, the weather was warm, and his remains were disposed of in the municipal dumping grounds.

CAN I USE YOUR CARMEX?

*T*he garage in Franklin, Wisconsin, where alchemist Alfred Woelbing first concocted Carmex in a ceramic warlock's pot, has been demolished, but you can still tour the plant to watch molten lip balm poured into the diminutive white jars of mythic proportions. You just can't get too close to the production line, as the secrets of the process are a closely held family secret. At ninety-five (perhaps Carmex cures the ravages of age as well as cold sores), Woelbing is still the active president of the company, although his son and grandson take care of the day-to-day details.

While many believe that Carmex use caused the sixties, it really was invented in 1936 and may therefore have caused the thirties, forties, and fifties as well (although the Second World War disrupted grease availability, the core of the product). Carmex, perhaps because of comedian Paula Poundstone's "Carmex addict" routines, is reported to contain an addictive agent (some suggest fiberglass or an acid that causes an itch continually needing to be soothed); but it is, as far as we can tell, mostly wax, camphor, alum, menthol, and a little salicylic acid thrown in for analgesic properties. This does not assuage the conspiracy-laden Web sites (check out alt.folklore.urban Carmex Addiction).

Since 1987 Carmex has also come in little tubes, but it's just not the same. Long-term addicts claim the mere sound of the tiny jar opening provides relief from a host of symptoms, including but not limited to chapped derma.

DAIRY SHRINE/HOARD MUSEUM
Fort Atkinson

William Dempster Hoard taught the gospel of dairy farming. The National Dairy Shrine, within the Hoard Historical Museum, exhibits such relics as cow clippers, tail holders, glass milk bottles with their little cardboard lids, butterfat testers, cream separators, and even a dog-powered butter churn.

Representing modern technology is a photo exhibit that details today's method of artificial insemination of dairy cattle, from collection to next generation. It makes another item on exhibit seem especially touching: the parachute that dropped semen from the air to breeders down below before the advent of frozen semen. It looks like a little silk parasol, and its precious package is wrapped in discreet plain brown paper (Hoard had great respect for cows and was well known for saying that one should "Speak to a cow as you would a lady"). A photograph of a very small

Artificial insemination of cattle used to be a chancy business. Sometimes the parachute that delivered the goods, like this one at the National Dairy Shrine, blew into the next county.

plane, the *Flying Bull*, and its barnstorming pilot completes the picture.

The Hoard Historical Museum has artifacts from the Blackhawk War, hundreds of arrowheads handsomely displayed, many mounted birds, including a passenger pigeon, and a horseskin rug with mane.

Located on U.S. Highway 12 East (Whitewater Avenue) within the city of Fort Atkinson. Open 9:30 A.M. to 3:30 P.M. Tuesday through Saturday, and 1:00 to 5:00 P.M. on the first Sunday of the month from September through May; 9:30 A.M. to 4:30 P.M. Tuesday through Saturday, and 1:00 to 5:00 P.M. Sunday in June, July, and August. No hours on Monday, ever. Call (414) 563–7769 for more details.

TEN CHIMNEYS
Genesee Depot

For decades Alfred Lunt and Lynn Fontanne were America's "First Couple" of the theater, and when they finished a long run on Broadway they came home to Genesee Depot. Here they could sit and stare or roam the fields. They could also play host to all their theatrical friends. Helen Hayes stayed here for a month or so every year. Eugene O'Neill worked on *Strange Interlude*. Noel Coward played the piano. Many others came and went—Charlie Chaplin, Laurence Olivier, Carol Channing, Katharine Hepburn, Julie Harris, Alexander Woollcott, S. N. Behrman, Robert Sherwood, Moss Hart—all right here in Genesee Depot.

Lunt had grown up in Milwaukee and loved the Wisconsin countryside. Over the years he acquired land, converted a chicken coop into a summer cottage, and added buildings

FLOSSIE'S BEST FRIEND

If Wisconsin does have more cows than people, it is only because they are encouraged to breed. And encouraging them to breed is the legacy of William D. Hoard of Fort Atkinson. Hoard was one of the first to speak of "cow temperament," something the rest of us in Dairyland have come to take for granted as a birthright.

Around the turn of the last century, Hoard wrote the dairy commandments:

Speak to a cow as you would to a lady.

Remember that a cow is a mother and her calf is a baby.

To him that loveth a cow, shall all other things be added—

feed, ensilage, butter, more grasses, more prosperity,

happier homes and greater wealth.

Hoard promoted the radical notions of the single-purpose milker; the building of silos; the testing of milk to protect against tuberculosis; and, in fact, transformed the farm in which several cows were kept into the modern dairy industry and the landscape of Wisconsin into the beautiful patchwork of dairy farms and fields you see today. Along the way he served in the Civil War; was elected governor of the state (as a Republican and Lincoln disciple, although ridiculed as the "cow candidate"); promoted the planting of alfalfa; brought Ag Science to the University of Wisconsin; made the farmer a political force to be reckoned with nationally; and founded Hoard's Dairyman, *the influential journal still published today.*

A statue of Hoard stands at the head of the agricultural campus at the University of Wisconsin–Madison, where you will want to be sure to stop at Babcock Hall to sample the ice cream and visit the dairy barns.

whose chimneys numbered ten and gave the estate its name.
Lunt was serious about his land. He grew strawberries, rasp-
berries, tomatoes, cucumbers, turnips, potatoes, and corn. He
made his own butter and bred cattle.

"The Fabulous Lunts" designed every room in the main
house like a stage set, fit for grand entrances and exits. They
engaged a set designer to cover the walls and ceilings with
elaborate murals. In one scene from the Old Testament, Adam
and Eve resemble each other because Fontanne posed for both.
Fond of old things, she said "Being in a modern house all the
rest of my life would be just like sitting nude forever in the
center of a huge white dinner plate." Artwork and antiques
from New York and Europe fill the rooms, which look pretty
much the way they did in the 1930s.

Lunt and Fontanne were married for fifty-five years, until
Lunt died in 1977. Fontanne stayed on at Ten Chimneys until
she died in 1983. It had been their permanent home since 1972,
their summer retreat since the 1920s.

Ten Chimneys Foundation is overseeing restoration of the
house and expects to reopen it in the spring of 2002. Call (262)
968–4161 for more information.

One of the most important advances in fountain-pen history was the invention of the mechanically filled pen by George Safford Parker of Janesville in 1904. Until then pens had been filled by using eyedroppers.

A WHITE BUFFALO
Janesville

Miracle, a white female buffalo, has been drawing crowds to her pasture ever since she was born on August 20, 1994. She is believed to be the first white buffalo calf born since 1933. Experts estimate the odds of that happening at one in 10 million. She has black eyes and is not an albino.

As a white calf, Miracle is important in the religious beliefs of many Native American peoples. Tribal elders say that the birth fulfills a sacred prophecy signaling a new age of global spirituality and unification of the races. They also told Miracle's owners, Dave and Val Heider and their son Corey, that the calf would turn black, red, and yellow—the other colors of the human race. Miracle completed those color changes in eleven months. When there is peace in the world, says the legend, Miracle will turn white again. Today she is still yellow, or blonde.

When news of the white calf spread, nearly a thousand people a day searched out the Heiders' farm and stood by the fence to see Miracle. Even the governor came to call. More than thirty tribes have performed nearly a hundred ceremonies in her honor. In 1998 Miracle gave birth to a calf, which was reddish in color. The youngster's name is Millennium.

To see Miracle at the Heiders' farm, go 4 miles west of I–90 on Avalon Road (exit 177) to the Rock River, then turn right on South River Road and go about a quarter-mile to 2739 South River Road. Open 10:00 A.M. to 5:00 P.M. daily. To sleep over with Miracle, right next to her pasture, call Buffalo Dude at (608) 752-2224 to make reservations for camping out. For a nominal fee the Heiders are offering a "rough-it type of thing" with cold running water, a camp fire, and a couple of buffalo steaks. Or visit Miracle at www.whitemiracle.com.

So That Barbershop Quartets Shall Not Perish from the Earth
Kenosha

The Society for the Preservation and Encouragement of Barbershop Quartet Singing in America makes its headquarters amid baronial splendor, in a Tudor Revival mansion overlooking Lake Michigan. Over the living-room fireplace (there are seven more) hangs a portrait not of Walter H. Alford, the Nash Motors executive who built the house (it even has a car wash), but of O. C. Cash, a Missouri boy who loved barbershops and close harmony. You can sink into the couch, which rests on Mr. Alford's $68,000 oriental carpet, and watch the whole story unfold on the video "A Walk through Harmony Hall."

Along the main staircase, with its stone balustrades, bronze banisters, and stained-glass panels of medieval court life, are photos of such quartets as the Bartlesville Barflies, the Four Hearsemen, and the Chord Busters. Outside the ballroom, now packed with electronic equipment, are museum exhibits. One tells the career story of a quartet from Wichita who sang at the wedding of Roy Rogers and Dale Evans; the newlyweds gave the singers a bronze statuette of Trigger as a memento of the day. It is here, along with pitch pipes and a historical survey of quartet fashion, from Wild West to leisure suits to today's formal wear.

The staff has been at home here for forty years and congenially receives the many visitors who roam the building and peer into their handsome offices. Alford Mansion, 6315 Third Avenue, is open year-round, 9:00 A.M. to 4:00 P.M. Monday through Friday. Group tours by appointment. Call (262) 653–8440 for more information.

*A flying saucer at rest on County Highway D
north of Belleville, where several UFO sightings were reported in the 1970s.
This one has a hatchway and running lights.*

FINALLY, AN OUTLET STORE FOR GUYS
Kenosha

There's no need for Dad to doze off in the parking lot at Prime Outlets while Mom and Sis are going nuts inside Donna Karan and J. Crew. On the opposite side of I–94 is the Kenosha Military Museum, an outdoor display of heavy equipment from World War I through Desert Storm—tanks, helicopters, landing craft . . . vehicles of all kinds in khaki tones.

The most conspicuous item is the huge Sky Crane, a heavy-lift helicopter that transported equipment in the Vietnam War. You can get behind the wheel of a Humvee (modern army jeep), a fast-attack vehicle (Desert Storm's version of a dune buggy), or a helicopter for a hands-on but stationary experience or photo op. For $25 you can go for a ride in a tank.

The vehicles on the lot aren't for sale, but the gift shop sells catalogs that can help make a dream of a Sherman tank in

In 1910 Cooper Underwear Company patented its Kenosha Klosed Krotch long underwear, and the following year it became the first underwear manufacturer to advertise in national magazines. In 1972 the Kenosha company changed its name to Jockey International.

your driveway come true. Open from 9:00 A.M. to 5:00 P.M.
Wednesday through Sunday year-round, except in inclement
weather. Located on the frontage road, County Q, about a mile
south of Highway 165 at I–94 (exit 374). Admission charge.
Call (262) 857–3418 for details.

A PYRAMID SCHEME?
Lake Mills

Lake Mills owes its nickname, the "City of Pyramids" (and
such local businesses as the Pyramid Driving School), to
three mysterious shapes at the bottom of Rock Lake.

In the nineteenth century Winnebagoes were telling the
early European settlers of Lake Mills about sunken "rock
tepees," and one day in 1900 two local duck hunters peered
down and saw them. Over the years fishermen and divers have
reported sighting something—and described an upside-down
ice-cream cone, or a Hershey's Chocolate Kiss, 20 or 30 feet
high and 100 feet long—but most of the time water conditions
have defied even high-tech video equipment. Are they manmade
or glacial debris? Some believe that pre-Columbian dwellers
built them on dry land before the area was flooded. Others say
that geology can explain the whole thing. The question
remains: archeological find of the century, or nature at work?

Those in the pyramid-builder camp point to large, flat-
topped pyramidal mounds a few miles east of Lake Mills.
Archeologists say that the people who lived here between about
A.D. 900 and 1200 built the mounds, plus a stockade of wooden
posts around their village. One mound had fire pits lined with
sand; another was for burials; a third was used for storing
corn. Portions of the stockade and two mounds have been
reconstructed at Aztalan State Park.

The unexplained underwater shapes are at the south end of Rock Lake. The archeological site is within Aztalan State Park and is listed in the National Registry of Historic Places. The park is located south of I–94 (exit 259) and is open daily from April through October.

After a hard storm in 1897, some Richland County farm boys discovered some huge bones poking out of a creek near the village of Boaz. Archeologists were all atwitter when the bones turned out to belong to a 9,000-year-old mastodon. The skeleton of the big bruiser now stands in the Geology Museum at the University of Wisconsin–Madison, 1215 Dayton Street. A two-dimensional plywood replica of the Boaz mastodon often appears in parades in Richland County on a Lions Club trailer. One side is painted to look like hair, the other side like bones.

ANCIENT FOSSILS IN THE CAPITOL
Madison

The yellow marble walls of the Hearing Room in the State Capitol Building contain dozens of ammonites, from the days when the future capitol site was sunk in a 70-million-year-old sea and giant snails made backroom deals. The ancient fossils look just like big snails.

You don't have to wait for a hearing on some burning issue to see them. Most of the time the Hearing Room is unoccupied and you're welcome to go in and look around. The ammonites are at eye level, and some of them are as large as 8 inches across.

When you leave the Hearing Room, head down the right side of the grand staircase and admire the starfish fossil on the fourth step from the bottom. It's about 400 million years old, and geologists say it's extremely rare. (Starfish lack the rigid skeleton necessary for preservation as fossils.)

At the bottom of the staircase, bear right toward the west wing and walk down the grand staircase to the ground floor. To the right of the bottom step is a cephalopod, about 20 inches long. This creature too is about 400 million years old; it lived in the sea, and, like the ammonite, had a hard body but a straight one, not coiled. You can see the breathing tube that ran down the length of its shell—it inhaled to sink, exhaled to rise. If you cross the rotunda to the south wing, you can see another cephalopod, or a chunk of one, on the floor between the two drinking fountains near the elevator on the east side.

The Hearing Room is in the north wing, second floor. The capitol is open daily from 7:00 A.M. to 8:00 P.M. Free guided tours of this glorious building are offered daily. Large groups should call ahead: (608) 266–0382. On a scale of one to ten, say state capitol junkies, this one is an eleven.

JEFFERSONIAN DEMOCRACY

*T*homas Jefferson never made it to Wisconsin (although his exploratory committee—Lewis, Clark, and Sacajawea—made it darn close). But his youngest son by Sally Hemings, his household slave at Monticello, did.

Eston Hemings Jefferson is buried in Madison's Forest Hills cemetery (on Speedway Road), along with his wife, Julia, and eight family members. Eston was the scion of a successful and well-respected Madison family that ran the Capital Hotel, a livery business that was active in early union associations. It was the DNA from John Jefferson, a descendant of Eston, which, through a match with a rare Y Jefferson chromosome, proved that Jefferson fathered eight children with Sally Hemings (herself the half-sister of his wife, while simultaneously her property), confirming what Eston never talked about: that his father was one of the Founding Fathers. Jefferson never formally freed his slaves but purportedly agreed to allow many to run away.

In 1836, at age twenty-eight, Eston fled to Ohio, and when the political tide turned against former slaves with the passage of the Fugitive Slave Act, he moved to the freshly minted state of Wisconsin in 1851. He married a black woman but lived as a white man, concealing his family history to his death in 1856. His brother Madison, who lived in Ohio, claimed the lineage to Jefferson in a biography and mentioned a brother in Wisconsin, though not by name, for his brother's well-being.

The 27-foot Wienermobile has a hot dog–shaped glove box and instrument panel, relish-colored seats, and storage space for up to 10,000 wiener whistles. Drivers of the six-wiener fleet are usually recent college graduates who must train at Hot Dog High in Madison, the home of Oscar Mayer Foods, before they get the keys to the five-ton wiener.

THE ANNALS OF TOILET PAPER
Madison

Several years ago Carol Kolb brought a roll of toilet paper home from the Trophy Room bar in Lodi, and since then her souvenir collection has grown to about 3,000 rolls. All fifty states are represented as well as such landmarks as the Statue of Liberty, Lambeau Field, the Alamo, Churchill Downs, Caesar's Palace, and Graceland. Many rolls are from foreign locations, such as the Vatican, and special exhibit areas are dedicated to Africa and Mexico.

The rolls are labeled with black marker pen (place, date, donor) and arranged in towers along the walls of a tiny living room in the apartment that Kolb shares with the museum's four-person board of directors. For acquisitions they depend on friends and, ever since the collection was mentioned in *Time* magazine, the kindness of strangers. The golden rule: "Never take the last roll."

In 1999 the Museum of Bathroom Tissue closed for remodeling, and the future of the collection as a museum remains uncertain.

The last guest checked out
years ago, but in better days the main office, shown here,
had keys for about twenty cabins. The cabins are still here, complete
with broken furniture, rusty TV sets, plumbing fixtures, and evidence
of visits from small creatures. On Highway 12 about 5 miles south of
Fort Atkinson.

OLE AND LENA

*Y*ou can have your Alphonse and Gaston. In Wisconsin there is no couple odder and more beloved than "Ole and Lena," the ribald married couple who are either Norwegian or Swedish, depending upon who's telling the story.

You could know a Badger for a really long time—even marry one—and never get around to bringing up the topic of sex. But for Ole, a rakish farmer who comes into his own when he meets, woos, and betroths the unrepressed Lena, mutual need leads to a match made in comedy heaven. Ole and Lena jokes are about half sexual innuendo and half opportunities to dig at either the Norsks or the Svensks, as appropriate.

While you can hear Ole and Lena jokes in cafes, churches, and Sons of Norway get-togethers in a broad band across Minnesota and Wisconsin, if you're looking for a sure thing, head to Stoughton, Wisconsin. Here the jokes are entirely at the expense of the Swedes. James P. Leary, in his book Midwestern Folk Humor, recalls that in the 1960s, the joke around that hotbed of student unrest, Madison, was "What do

you get when you cross lutefisk with a hit of LSD? A trip
to Stoughton."

Just a few miles south of
Madison on Highway 51, head
for Fosdal Home Bakery on
Main Street, but first familiarize
yourself with and be prepared to
recite in your best Fargo lilt this Leary-recorded joke,
"Ole and Lena's First Date":

So he asked her for a date. "Yah," she'd go out with
him.

He said, "Would you like to have a cigarette?"

She said, "No, I can't have a cigarette. What would I
tell my Sunday school class?"

"Well," he said, "would you take a drink?"

"No, I can't have a drink. What would I tell my
Sunday school class?"

He said, "Lena, will you go home and spend the
night with me?"

She said, "Yah, that I will do."

So the next morning, he said, "Lena, what are you
going to tell your Sunday school class now?"

"Well, yust the same thing I've been telling them for
years and years: 'You don't have to smoke and drink to
have fun.'"

COWS   ON   THE   CAMPUS
Madison

There's a strange sight at the Dairy Cattle Instruction and Research Center at the University of Wisconsin—cows with portholes in their sides. It's in the interest of science, a means of observing digestive processes. The cows don't appear to mind, and the dairy-science people assure us that they don't.

If you get up bright and early or stop by the center late in the afternoon, you can stand at a big picture window and watch cows being milked. Then, if you ask, you can go backstage and look for the cows with the portholes. If you're lucky, maybe someone with a good reason to want to know what's going on in there will come along, remove the plug-style porthole, reach inside, and pull out some stomach contents.

The Dairy Research Center is at 1815 Linden Drive, just a few doors down from the busy Babcock Dairy Store, which sells ice cream, cheese, and butter made from the milk of these very cows.

Arthur D. Hasler is credited with solving one of the great mysteries of salmon migration in 1945. As a professor of zoology at University of Wisconsin–Madison, he hypothesized that salmon use their sense of smell to find their way home. He proved it by collecting salmon, stuffing cotton up the noses of some of them, and sending them back downstream. The ones without the cotton found their way straight off; the ones with cotton got confused and made mistakes.

E N T O M O L O G I Z E R   A N D   C R I C K E T   S P I T T E R
M a d i s o n

Dan Capps holds the world's record in cricket spitting. First he won the Bug Bowl Cricket-Spitting Contest at Purdue University, where he was exhibiting his insect collection. Then, to satisfy Guinness's tough standards, he repeated the deed on its "World Records Prime Time" television show in Hollywood. His official distance is 32 feet ½ inch.

A competition cricket is dead, limp, and mushy, having been frozen and thawed.

Dan's personal insect collection contains tens of thousands of insects—wasps, beetles, moths, butterflies, dragonflies, and, of course, crickets—with an emphasis on tropical species. It's an enormous collection for an amateur (he earns his livelihood as a mechanic at Oscar Mayer). Dan's knowledge of insects is self-taught, and he often shows and talks about wonders of the insect world at schools and elsewhere. (His own fascination with insects began in grade school when the principal opened a cigar box and showed Dan his luna and cecropia moths.) Dan sees his school visits as a chance to open eyes to diversity in nature and to enlighten—people who shriek at the sight of an insect the size of a baseball, for instance, learn that large insects often are harmless. A well-respected collector, he also gets invitations to address entomologists' professional meetings.

Dan's own person further testifies to the significance of ecology in his life. Two artist friends designed a tapestry of images from nature—his favorite butterflies, insects, and flowers—that is tattooed over his upper body (but it doesn't extend below his elbows—that is, the tattoo insects don't make an appearance at his "Introduction to Insects" visits at grade schools).

For more information write or call Dan Capps at P.O. Box 8216, Madison, WI 53708, (608) 332–5434.

GOOD GRIEF
Middleton

I n a time of great personal loss, it's a comfort to know that your undertaker has embalmed chipmunks in a topless-bar display.

Sam Sanfillippo displays his enormous collection of taxidermied wildlife downstairs at the funeral home that bears his name. It takes four large rooms here to contain the hundreds of fish, birds, and animals he has hunted or otherwise acquired, and there are more at home. As a teenager he caught the gigantic marlin on the wall, which is almost eclipsed by all that followed.

He and his personal Northwoods taxidermist obviously have had fun dreaming up settings for subjects. At the "Woodland Fair," several chipmunks ride a merry-go-round, while others in skirts of gold upholstery fringe perform at the "topless girlie show." Albino squirrels shoot baskets at a Fisher-Price hoop or pose in shocking-pink convertibles. Gray squirrels line up for refills at a Northwoods bar.

Interesting stories are behind many of the acquisitions. The wild boar charged out of the brush in the backwoods of Georgia. The two tiny fawns were found inside a doe that had been hit by a car. The albino squirrels came from a park in St. Louis. The three-legged goose, the blonde raccoons, and the paddle-nosed catfish are rarities.

Photographs of Sanfillippo with presidents, governors, and astronauts offer another dimension of his long and full life. And the animals speak for themselves.

Visitors are welcome, but call first: (608) 238–8406. Sanfillippo Cress Funeral Home is at 6021 University Avenue.

A SECRET TUNNEL
Milton

Joseph Goodrich was an innkeeper, a devout Seventh Day Baptist, and such a staunch abolitionist that he dug a 50-foot tunnel between his log cabin and his inn to aid fugitive slaves as they traveled the "Underground Railroad" to freedom. When runaways found their way to the cabin, Goodrich lifted the secret trapdoor to the secret tunnel that led to the secret room in the basement. There they could hide and rest up for the next leg of the perilous journey.

The Underground Railroad of the nineteenth century was not, of course, a real railroad, and this seems to be the only part of it that actually was underground.

The inn was Milton House, and upstairs from the secret room, guests were resting up after a hard day's stagecoach ride. Sojourner Truth was once a guest, and although she and Goodrich saw eye to eye on abolition, they disagreed on smoking. Sojourner Truth smoked a pipe, and Goodrich told her that she wouldn't get to heaven because smoking made her breath bad. She said she wouldn't need her breath in heaven.

Grout fanciers may be interested to know that Milton House is the oldest poured-grout structure in the United States.

Goodrich was one of Milton's first settlers (and therefore didn't have to worry about neighbors who might wonder why he was digging that tunnel), having arrived in March 1839 with his family after a thirty-four-day trip by covered wagon from Alfred, New York—a hotbed of the abolitionist movement. He constructed the inn in 1844, and when it was finished, the *Janesville Gazette* described it as "truly an object of curiosity." It was in the shape of a hexagon and had a chimney in the middle so that each room could have its own stove and stovepipe connection to the chimney.

In 1998 the National Park Service officially recognized the Milton House Museum as a National Historic Landmark for its role in the Underground Railroad. The museum is located at the intersection of Highways 26 and 59. Guided tours daily from 10:00 A.M. to 5:00 P.M. Memorial Day through Labor Day (school tours by arrangement at other times of year). Admission charge. Call (608) 868–7772 for more information.

NEXT TIME USE IT TO THINK
Milwaukee

The world's largest dinosaur skull is on display at the Milwaukee Public Museum, at the far end of the rest of its reconstructed skeleton. The big guy is a Torosaurus, discovered in 1981 in the Hell Creek Badlands of northeastern Montana.

The fossil is also the first Torosaurus discovered with accompanying skeletal material, including leg bones. Because the skeleton was not complete, missing bones had to be fabricated from fiberglass. The museum did not want the Torosaurus, which means "bull lizard," to be just a pretty face (like some reconstructions elsewhere), so to help visitors appreciate the reconstruction process, it painted the replicated material white and left the original fossil remains their natural brown color. The work was done in full public view by a team of dedicated volunteers.

The museum is in downtown Milwaukee at 800 West Wells Street. Open daily 9:00 A.M. to 5:00 P.M. Admission fee. More information is available at www.mpm.edu or by calling (414) 278–2700.

MILWAUKEE TALKING

*I*n Milwaukee *"Come by the house later"* does not mean that the speaker is expecting you to make an offer on the duplex, nor does it imply that the addressee will not be invited in. It's just how you ask somebody over. Although if you can't wait to be asked, you can still station yourself under a friend's window and yell *"Call for Steve-ee!"* if, in fact, it's Stevie you want to see.

Milwaukee's German argot (further complicated in my family with Yiddish-isms) makes *"bubblers"* out of drinking fountains, finds *"icebox"* still the preferred term for refrigerator, and *"ain'a?"* the way to conclude a declarative sentence. (*"Follow me?"* my dad's preferred closer, is another favorite.)

While it may not be true that Milwaukee nearly entered the war on the German side, *"Cream City"* syntax owes a lot to loose—or literal—translations from the German and, on the South Side, the Polish. *"Milwaukee Talk,"* a pamphlet originally published by the Milwaukee Journal in the 1950s (and cited in James P. Leary's Wisconsin Folklore) is an invaluable primer for wannabe Milwaukeeans:

> *"It's warm in here. Why don't you run up the window?"*
> *"From the refrigerator get the eggs and I will fry you."*
> *"Don't nervous me, I get easy mad."*
> *"Come broom off the snow, the sidewalk is getting thick."*
> *"I gotta clean my hairs, they're so greasy."*

Naturally, to poetry it lends itself:

I give to you a violet
In token of I'm glad we met
I hope we may already yet
Once more again together get.

So stop in at Goldmann's (page 150) and have a coffee cup and a pie slice.

WHEN MILWAUKEE WAS YOUNG
Milwaukee

People come to the Bay View neighborhood from all over to fill their water jugs from the spigots of the last artesian well left in the city. This has been going on for more than a century. No one has determined the source of the water, but the city tests it once a month and declares it to be safe.

Some people claim that the iron-flavored water has curative powers and drink it for whatever ails them. Others, possibly fearing that the detergents at automatic carwashes are too harsh for the duct tape that holds their car together, slosh on a few gallons from the well. At least that's what one man was doing to his 1978 Le Baron last January in eight-degree weather.

The well is located on Pryor Avenue between Superior Street and Wentworth Avenue, about 2 blocks from Lake Michigan. It's a concrete structure approximately 5 feet tall, in a friendly setting of wooden benches and (in season) flowers.

HOME OF THE OOF OOF POLKA
Milwaukee

Art Altenburg yearned for a concertina when he was a boy. To help him earn the money, his father, a farmer, gave him a quarter-acre of land. The number of rocks and roots that Art first had to clear out are forever engraved in his memory, but eventually he was able to grow and sell enough cucumbers to the local pickle factory to earn the $60 he needed for the concertina. Today he has thirty-five concertinas (accordions with buttons for keys) on the back bar of Art Altenburg's Concertina Bar, and more at home.

Art's place is actually a whole concertina universe, and hundreds come here on weekends for polka music and dancing. On Friday and Saturday nights a hired band—such as Karl and the Country Dutchmen from Minnesota—comes to play. (Art used to have his own group, the Jolly Jacks Concertina Orchestra, and has composed a few numbers of his own, such as "The Oof Oof Polka.") Locals turn up on Thursday nights for jam sessions.

There's no taxidermy in this bar. Instead, the walls are covered with brass instruments, photographs of polka bands and concertina players, and awards such as "Wisconsin Polka Entertainment Center Operator of the Year, 1994."

Art's Concertina Bar, 1920 South Thirty-seventh Street, off Burnham Avenue, opens at 11:00 A.M. weekdays. Closed Sunday. Music goes from 9:00 P.M. to 1:00 A.M. Friday, 9:00 P.M. to 1:30 A.M. Saturday. Call (414) 384–2570 for more details.

On June 13, 1998, an estimated 50,000 bikes rode in a 10-mile-long parade through Milwaukee to celebrate Harley-Davidson's ninety-fifth anniversary. By the time the Hogs come back for the centennial in 2003, the Harley-Davidson Experience Center, an interactive museum, will be open in what was once the Schlitz brewery.

AND SOME REALLY ANCIENT PIN BOYS
Milwaukee

From the outside Holler House looks like about a thousand other corner taverns in Milwaukee, but beyond the door at the end of the bar and down the stairs is bowling history: the oldest alleys (all two of them) in the nation.

The American Bowling Congress sanctioned them in 1910, and they're very much in use today. See the bowling bags lined up in the "locker room"—two long shelves under the front window. Some regulars have been coming for forty years. Bowlers sacrifice fifteen or twenty points to play here. It's disorienting to bowl in a tunnel instead of a thirty-lane alleyrama, on hardwood instead of synthetic lanes, with balls that come rumbling back in full view from human pin setters busily scampering around back there.

Photos of bowling teams confirm the history—upstanding-looking guys wearing white shirts and neckties and representing Ryczek Embalmers, Miller High Life, La Dora Cigars. Fourth-generation owner Marcy Skowronski knows the neighborhood stories that go with them. She also can explain another feature of the Holler House decor: brassieres autographed by their owners, dangling in bunches from various fixtures.

Holler House, 2042 West Lincoln, opens for business at 4:00 P.M. every day except Monday. Call to inquire about bowling (414–647–9284), and watch for scenes filmed at Holler House in the movie *Chump Change*.

WHY MILWAUKEE
FEELS BADLY

John Schrank, a bartender, convinced that Theodore Roosevelt intended to establish a monarchy by running for a third term, stalked him for 2,000 miles before putting a bullet in him in Milwaukee in 1912. It didn't help that William McKinley had appeared to him in a dream pointing to Roosevelt as McKinley's murderer—which, in Schrank's mind, was more portentous than just something he had eaten before retiring.

Fortunately for Roosevelt, the length of his speech may have saved his life. The bullet had to pass through the doubled-up bulk of a fifty-page speech as well as a case for the metal spectacles he needed to read it. In true Bull Moose fashion, he railed for an hour with the bullet lodged 5 inches into his chest, where, having missed all major organs and arteries, it was to remain for the rest of his life. Roosevelt said, "I don't want Milwaukee to feel badly about this," which has come to be the city's unofficial motto since October 14, 1912. Still, he was removed to Chicago's Mercy Hospital for treatment, even though Mt. Sinai was just down the street.

Teddy was actually shot leaving his hotel on the way to the Milwaukee Auditorium; it was on the ride there that an aide noticed the hole in the president's overcoat. Asking only for a clean handkerchief to stem the blood flow, Roosevelt launched into his stump speech, during which it became clear to his audience that something was dreadfully wrong.

Schrank was eventually confined to the Hospital for the Criminally Insane in Oshkosh, and Roosevelt lost his bid for a third term to Woodrow Wilson, suffering lifelong debilities from the wound (complicated by untreated malaria from a subsequent rafting trip in the Amazon; the man did not know from convalescing).

For years Milwaukee suffered image problems due to the assassination attempt. It had nearly recovered when a Milwaukee lad, Arthur Bremer, undid it all by shooting George Wallace in 1972.

REMEMBER TO FIRST GET YOUR
GRAPEFRUIT DRILLED
Milwaukee

If your bowling score suffered at Holler House, you'll feel a
lot better about it at Koz's. According to comments in the
visitors' book that Duwayne Kosakoski keeps at the bar, his
customers are positively thrilled with the totals they rack up in
the next room. It seems to help that the game here is miniature
bowling. The four alleys are only 16 feet long, the pins are 9
inches high, and the ball is akin to a four-pound grapefruit.

At one time mini-bowling was a major pastime in Milwaukee; today Koz's offers the only game in town. "The most hon-
est bowling in America is at Koz's Mini-Bowl," wrote Frank
Deford in *Sports Illustrated,* where "almost anybody can bowl a
300. Many folks in the area do their bowling only at Koz's,
because the company is good, the beer is cold, and there's hard
truth enough in the rest of the world."

Bowling hours are not during school hours, because school
kids set the pins; not Thursday, because that's league night for
eight men's teams; and not when the Packers are playing on
television. Travelers from all over the world have searched out
Koz's Mini-Bowl and Bar and mixed with the neighborhood
regulars at 2078 South Seventh Street (at Becher). Call (414)
383–0560 for more information.

*This house was built in 1926
from plans for a ship, by a salesman who dreamed of
sailing the high seas. White with blue trim and a 30-foot lighthouse off the
starboard bow, the one-bedroom Edmund B is at the corner of North
Cambridge Avenue and East Hampshire Street, near the University of
Wisconsin–Milwaukee campus.*

J U R A S S I C   R E T A I L
M i l w a u k e e

Goldmann's and Dretzka's department stores are two examples of the *Milwaukee Journal*'s statement in 1998 that "retro may be hot now but in Milwaukee it never went out of style." These stores seem to have changed hardly a whit in the past century.

Goldmann's is especially beloved for its World Famous Diner, which serves breakfast, lunch, and dinner at three U-shaped counters. Waitresses from central casting serve such classics as the Meatloaf Dinner ($3.99) and the Incredible Malt ($1.49). The size of the malt requires that the metal container it was created in arrive alongside the glass that holds the first serving (partly because whipped cream occupies the top few inches). Formica counter, chrome stools, and six-tier pie cases complete the picture.

Liberace, born Wladziu Valentino Liberace in West Allis, attended West Milwaukee High School, where he almost always won first prize for "Most Original Costume" on Character Day. At various times he was Haile Selassie, Yankee Doodle Dandy, and Greta Garbo. At age fourteen he presented his first piano recital at Wisconsin College of Music, and at twenty he soloed with the Chicago Symphony Orchestra, under the name Walter Buster Keys.

Dretzka's has no lunch counter, but it has merchandise that would be hard to find anywhere else. There are jingle bells on cards, buttons in boxes, a wide selection of plastic rain bonnets—plain, with daisies, or with Wonder Bread dots—replacement inserts for your metal box of watercolors with ovals in such shades as orchid and mustard, and so much more (especially clothing). If you're looking for something specific in this large store, however, it would be wise to ask. You wouldn't think to look for the rubber chickens, for instance, between the insoles and the zippers, but that is where they are.

Goldmann's has merchandise, too—three floors of clothing and housewares and a mezzanine of colorful, kitschy lamps.

Goldmann's and Dretzka's are on the south side of Milwaukee. Goldmann's, 930 West Mitchell, is open weekdays at 9:00 A.M. and closes at 5:30 P.M. every day except Friday, when it closes at 8:00 P.M. It's also open from 11:00 A.M. to 4:00 P.M. the first Sunday of the month. Dretzka's, 4746 South Packard Avenue, Cudahy, is open 9:00 A.M. to 5:00 P.M. Monday through Saturday, closed Sunday.

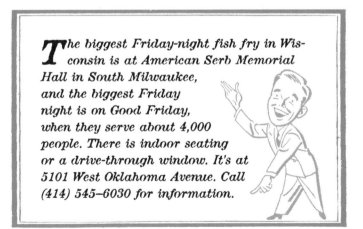

The biggest Friday-night fish fry in Wisconsin is at American Serb Memorial Hall in South Milwaukee, and the biggest Friday night is on Good Friday, when they serve about 4,000 people. There is indoor seating or a drive-through window. It's at 5101 West Oklahoma Avenue. Call (414) 545–6030 for information.

STINKS SO GOOD
Monroe

Chalet Cheese Co-op is the only factory in this country that makes the notoriously funky-smelling limburger. Fifty years ago about 100 plants made limburger, but tastes change, and now Chalet Cheese stands alone.

The Chalet Cheese Co-op doesn't offer tours, T-shirts, or tasting parties. It does, however, have a store that sells its products (limburger, brick, and baby Swiss). In an adjoining room you can see the decidedly low-tech, labor-intensive packaging operation: three or four women in white seated at a table wrapping little blocks of limburger in rectangles of parchment paper, then waxed paper, and finally foil. The one million pounds of limburger they wrap annually are sold throughout the United States under various labels; so if you buy domestic limburger, it came from *here*.

The store is open from 7:00 A.M. to 3:30 P.M. Monday through Friday, 8:00 A.M. to 1:30 P.M. Saturday. Chalet Cheese Co-op is located at N4858 County Road N (a rollercoaster-style road) about 4 miles north of Monroe. Call (608) 325–4343 for more information.

Limburger is generally associated with practical jokes and sandwiches, and the best place to appreciate the latter—on buttered toast with a slice of sweet onion and a little honey—is Baumgartner's Tavern in Monroe. Baumgartner's believes there's not a place in the world that sells more limburger sandwiches, and tradition probably accounts for that distinction. Further reminders of the area's Swiss heritage appear in the form of huge oil paintings of alpine scenes; nearly half a mountain goat, among other hunting trophies; and local guys playing cards—as well as a photo of Miss Limburger of 1998 in a recent Cheese Days parade.

Baumgartner's Cheese Store and Tavern is on the west side of the Green County Courthouse Square. Hours are 8:00 A.M. to bar time, seven days a week. Call (608) 325–6157 for details.

HAPPY HERDSMEN
Monroe

For almost fifty years radio station WEKZ in Monroe has broadcast a program of Swiss music. "Let's Yodel" and "Us Herdsmen Are Happy" are some of the tunes heard by listeners in three states—Iowa and Illinois, as well as Wisconsin—six days a week.

Martha Bernet, who took over for the original host in 1956, opens the show by greeting the audience and announcing the songs in Swiss and then English. She tapes the show from her own albums, tapes, and CDs, which she has collected over the course of many trips back home; and she balances the show among singing, yodeling, and instrumental. Martha and her husband, a cheesemaker, came to this country from Switzerland in 1947 and later opened a cheese and sausage shop in Monroe. She also yodels and plays accordion.

The "Swiss Program" is heard from 1:05 to 1:35 P.M. Sunday through Friday on WEKZ (1260 AM).

One summer day in 1909, Ole Evinrude purchased ice cream for a picnic, but by the time he rowed across Okauchee Lake in Waukesha County to the picnic site, the sweet stuff had melted. His disappointment led to his inventing "the detachable rowboat motor" and organizing Evinrude Motor Company.

The tin man of Highway 78 awaits his friend the rural mail carrier. Farther down the driveway is 13-foot-high Peg Leg Pete, a pirate with rail spikes for teeth and a frying pan for an eye patch. Located about halfway between Black Earth and Mount Horeb.

Poupon U
Mount Horeb

The night in 1986 that the Boston Red Sox lost the World
Series, Wisconsin's Assistant Attorney General Barry Leven-
son was distraught. Seeking comfort in food, he went to an all-
night supermarket and had an epiphany in the condiment
aisle: "When I stood before the mustards, a voice spoke to me:
'If you collect us, they will come.'"

The collection began in the basement of his home and moved
to a pump house in the back yard. One Saturday morning several years later, with the help of a "Pass the Mustard" human
chain, it was moved into a store a few blocks away on Main
Street.

As of Mustard Day 1999, the museum had 3,232 jars of
mustard from all over the world, a fine display of antique mustard pots, mustard-in-music items, and many other things
mustard. The Mustard Piece Theater runs the video "Mustard:
The Spice of Nations."

Annual events include a reunion of people named Mustard;
National Mustard Day early in August; and Elm Farm Ollie
Day in February, in honor of the first cow to fly in an airplane
(it's the Dairyland connection). If nothing else, the Mustard
Museum proves that you can promote anything.

Mount Horeb Mustard Museum, 109 East Main Street, is
open from 10:00 A.M. to 5:00 P.M. daily (closed Wednesday in
January and February). Give them a call at (608) 437–3986.

*The Tourist Troll is one of several
trolls from Scandinavian folklore along the Trollway
of downtown Mount Horeb. Michael J. Feeney is the artist.*

JA, DAS IST EINE DUNCE CAP
New Glarus

O n May 13, 1845, two valleys' worth of villagers—fewer than 200 people in all—from the Swiss canton of Glarus said farewell to Europe forever and sailed for America. On June 18 they ran out of potatoes; on July 19—by now aboard a riverboat on the Ohio—they were attacked by bloodthirsty mosquitoes. But in Galena, Illinois, they were reunited with the advance guard, two men who had been sent to scout for a place comparable to home and found it in Green County, Wisconsin. Together they walked the last 60 miles.

The soil was rich, water was plentiful, the landscape sort of resembled Switzerland, and the price was right—$1.25 per acre. On July 17, 1845, they purchased 1,280 acres and called their new village New Glarus.

The Swiss Historical Village consists of fourteen buildings that tell the rest of the story. A family of eight lived in the authentic 14- by 16-foot log cabin. In the one-room church, they endured two-hour sermons. The 1880 general store displays standard merchandise as well as examples of what an irrepressible Swiss can do with a sharp knife: intricate memorials carved from beeswax, cathedral-like superstructures of wood, a necklace of fruit pits.

Among other heavy-duty equipment in the blacksmith shop is a *schnitzelbank*, the very one in question in the hearty drinking song that asks *"Ist das nicht eine schnitzelbank? Ja, das ist eine schnitzelbank. . . ."* The fully equipped, original one-room *schul haus* even has a dunce cap—not just some flimsy cone-thing fashioned from a piece of notebook paper but a sturdy, deadly serious dunce cap. The print shop has all the equipment needed to print the *New Glarus Post* and, among other news clips, Mrs. T. C. Hefty's 20-column-inch recipe for soap: "Dissolve one can Eagle brand lye in one quart of cold rain water. . . ."

Further examples of doing things the hard way appear in a building full of farm implements. The ice-harvesting plow implies no rest for the weary farmer, even after he had hung up his corn binder and hay knives for the winter. The village would not, of course, be complete without a cheese factory, of which Green County had 200 a century ago.

Knowledgeable local guides conduct the tours and add interesting asides about their relatives. The Swiss Historical Village, 612 Seventh Avenue, is open daily 9:00 A.M. to 4:30 P.M. from May 1 through October 31. Admission charge. Call (608) 527–2317 for more information.

THE HILLS ARE ALIVE WITH THE SOUND OF ALPHORNS
New Glarus

Those goats frolicking in the meadows on the outskirts of New Glarus weren't put there by the chamber of commerce. Nor were those silky brown Swiss cows grazing along Highway 69. This is the real thing, a town of chalet-style buildings and red geraniums that was settled by emigrants from Switzerland whose descendants perpetuate some unusual traditions. It even has a yodel club, the only one in America, which is responsible not only for much of the yodeling that goes on at festivals but also the alphorn blowing and flag throwing.

One longtime resident has remarked that New Glarus is almost more Swiss than Switzerland.

The Heidi Festival in June offers ethnic entertainment and three performances of a play about Heidi, one of them in

Leon Varjian led the
Boom Box Parade around the capitol in Madison in 1983 to
the tune of "Stars and Stripes Forever," courtesy of station
WORT. The fifty band members wore red jackets; the mayor
wore a black tuxedo.

German. The Wilhelm Tell Festival in September offers similar entertainment, substituting an outdoor drama (also in both English and German) about the folk hero for the play about the girl with braids. For more information about New Glarus call (800) 527–6838.

LOOK WHAT I FOUND WITH THE DUST BUNNIES!

Oconomowoc

It's supposed to be good luck to find a cat whisker, so over the years Pauline Bemis got in the habit of picking up a whisker if she happened to see one lying there. She placed each one on a little shelf behind the glass door of a grandfather clock, and by now she has a large bundle of cat whiskers, hundreds of them.

The cats that she has owned over the past fifteen years are all represented in the collection: Little Caesar, Figaro, Zachary Robert, Pepper, Mitzie, Tiger, and Blackie. On average a cat probably has twenty-four whiskers, twelve on each side of the nose.

Pauline also has a large rock collection, which was featured at the Oconomowoc Public Library. Just for fun, she included the cat whiskers in the exhibit. Did people ask a lot of questions about the rocks? Not really. They were more curious about the cat whiskers.

Pauline has never counted them and has too many other things to do to sit around counting cat whiskers. Though semiretired, she teaches about woodwind instruments at two schools, gives private lessons, repairs instruments, and directs a hand-bell choir at church. In 1999 she received Oconomowoc's annual civic award in recognition of her musical involvement and other volunteer efforts.

THE DWARFS HAVE NEVER BEEN SMALLER
Pardeeville

I magine holding in one field of vision the Jefferson Memorial, Niagara Falls, the House of the Seven Dwarfs, the Taj Mahal, and a New England seacoast village! Such an experience lies only 20 miles east of I–90/94. It's La Reau's World of Miniature Buildings, the work of a retired school principal and a school-teacher, Paul and Clarice La Reau. They've been carving famous places on a scale of ½ inch = 1 foot, with Styrofoam and hot

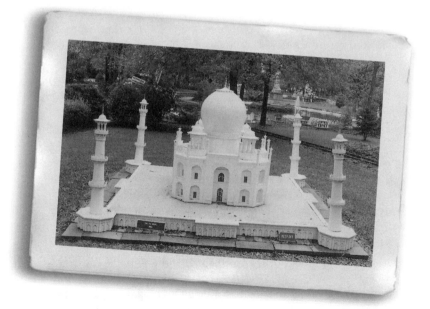

The Taj Mahal of Pardeeville, with windmill,
Statue of Liberty, and New England seacoast village in the background.

wires, since 1972. Their creations are all laid out on curving garden walks next to their ranch house a mile south of town.

An awesome amount of work and faithfulness to detail are represented here. The little landmarks (with hours of building time) include the U.S. Capitol (1,487 hours), Mount Rushmore (67), Mount Vernon (128), Monticello (144), the Lincoln Memorial (585), Neuschwanstein Castle (359), and Chartres Cathedral (9,764 hours). Another area, with a mystical mood, offers Stonehenge, the Great Pyramids, the Sphinx of Egypt, Buddha, and the Great Wall of China. There's also one called Life of Christ.

La Reau's World of Miniature Buildings is on Highway 22 south of Pardeeville, between Highways 33 and 16. Open 10:00 A.M. to 5:00 P.M. daily from Memorial Day through September. Admission charge. Call (608) 429–2848 for details.

SPEED SITTING, I MEAN,
SEED SPITTING
Pardeeville

Various talents are useful at Pardeeville's Watermelon Festival. Those with oral gifts can enter the United States Watermelon-Eating and Seed-Spitting Championships. Those with artistic talents can enter the melon-sculpture contest.

Spitting contestants select their seeds from the official wedges, toe the starting line, and wind up, so to speak, as officials with measuring tapes scamper to record the distance. A recent first-place winner of the Men's Open spat his seed 36 feet 3 inches. Eating contestants sit at picnic tables, bury their

SMELT-O-RAMA

*I**f you're not from around here, you might find it odd
to see grown men in snowmobile suits hanging over a
bridge at night, lowering large nets on pulleys and shin-
ing flashlights into the water. But after you live here a
while, you might not only think nothing of it, you might
join them!*

*It's smelting! (Pronounced with a "sh-" for complete
authenticity.) Don't let the fact that they're biting the
heads off the live little fish put you off; that merely
appeases the smelt gods to ensure a good harvest. The
smelt start running to spawn in mid-April (at night, of
course; no one likes to be seen spawning) in Lake Michigan and in inland lakes across Wisconsin. You've got to
eat the tails, although the heads are optional, according
to local custom. They come one way: battered, deep
fried, and washed down with beer, although some folks
like to slide 'em down with horseradish, hot sauce, tar-
tar sauce, or, I know, beer. They're delicious, but you've
got to eat a lot of them.*

*Curious? To give them a try, head for downtown
Port Washington on the first weekend after Easter. The
Van Ells-Schanern Post 82 American Legion
(414–284–4690) typically feeds more than a ton of smelt
to some 2,000 or 3,000 aficionados—it's a fundraiser, so
you can feel good about it. Bring your own coolers of
beer, and butter and condiments, if needed. The smelt
feast takes place at the Memorial Building in Lake
Park, on the lakefront.*

*Whatever you do, remember the tails (or the tail
patrol will get you), and don't even think of asking for
the batter recipe—it's a secret. But odds are beer helps
it cling.*

An aquarium of rare
watermelon fish at the festival in Pardeeville.

heads in their watermelon wedges, and await the starting signal. The best eating time in 1999 was four and a half seconds.
In the 1999 melon-sculpture contest, the theme of the first-
place winner was "Jonah and the Whale."

No one has to compete to eat, and tons of watermelon are
served free to all. Second Sunday in September in Chandler
Park, just north of the business district.

R ETURN   OF   THE   T WO - H EADED   P IG
P o y n e t t e

The MacKenzie Environmental Center made headlines in
May 1999 when the two-headed pig disappeared from its
Aliens Museum. The pig was kept in a one-gallon jar filled
with formaldehyde, displayed alongside some of nature's other
curiosities. As a sign at the museum entrance gently explains
to visiting schoolchildren, OCCASIONALLY IN NATURE ABNORMAL
PLANTS AND ANIMALS OCCUR.

"Nothing is sacred," said the sheriff, and announced a
$1,000 reward for information through the Crimestoppers tip
line. Two farmers who each happened to have two-bodied, one-
headed pigs in jars called to offer them to the museum. "It
was real nice of them," said the sheriff. Finally, more than
three weeks later, the pig was found on a hiking trail. Sheriff's deputies rushed it to Divine Savior Hospital in Portage to
top off the formaldehyde and returned it to the museum.
Today the pig is again in the display case that it shares with a
four-legged pheasant and a Siamese raccoon.

Other exhibits at the Aliens Museum show a white wood-
chuck, a white gray squirrel, a white white-tailed deer, a white
flatheaded catfish, a white porcupine (examples of albinism); a
black red fox, a black gray squirrel (melanism); and a one-
antlered deer skull (hermaphroditism).

MacKenzie Environmental Education Center, W7303
County Highway CS, off Highway Q east of Poynette, occupies
280 acres and features wildlife exhibits, museums, and hiking
trails. The grounds are open from dawn to dusk year-round

except during deer gun season; wildlife exhibit and museums are open daily 8:00 A.M. to 4:00 P.M. May 1 to mid-October; 8:00 A.M. to 4:00 P.M. Monday through Friday in winter; closed on winter holidays. Call (608) 635–8110 for information.

THE CHICAGO TYPEWRITER
Racine

In the middle of the afternoon on November 20, 1933, John Dillinger and five henchmen entered American Trades Bank at Fifth and Main in downtown Racine and told everybody to reach for the sky. An exhibit in the lobby of the Racine Police Station tells what happened after that. Dillinger and his gang took $27,000—and, for their getaway, a policeman's .45-caliber Thompson machine gun and two human shields, the bank president and a bookkeeper.

The exhibit includes the Tommy gun, which was recovered later with *John Dillinger* etched into the stock, and elaborates on the gun's role in bootleggers' drive-by shootings and its vivid nickname, the "Chicago Typewriter." It also contains the black shoestrings that the gang used to tie the bank president and the bookkeeper to a tree somewhere in Waukesha County. Shoestrings? The exhibit says they were donated to the Kenosha County Historical Museum by the bookkeeper, Ursula Patzke.

Apparently Dillinger made the most of his few years on Earth. He stole forty-one chickens from Homer Zook at age twenty, spent nine years in prison for robbing an elderly grocer, worked his way up to "Public Enemy Number One," and was gunned down at age thirty-one. His WANTED description and set of prints are here, too.

The Police Department is at 730 Center Street (Highway 32) in downtown Racine. The bank is now an M&I bank.

*A Frank Lloyd Wright–
designed white elephant, the Research Tower
at the S.C. Johnson headquarters in Racine. It has been
standing empty for about thirty years because it doesn't
meet safety codes.*

PRAIRIE-STYLE, BUCKET INCLUDED

"**W**ingspread," a spectacular Frank Lloyd Wright house of the 1930s, has a fireplace with an opening tall enough for 12-foot logs to stand on end vertically. This innovative design proved impractical because logs burn from the bottom and eventually fall out into the room. Another inventive feature was the disappearing table. At the end of each course, the kitchen staff could pull the table into the kitchen, prepare it for the next course, and slide it back out to the dinner guests. Like some other Wright buildings, at first it had a leaky roof. Wright responded to complaints with "That's how you can tell it's a roof," "That's what happens when you leave a work of art out in the rain," and "Move your chair." The Johnson Foundation operates Wingspread as a conference facility. It is on Lighthouse Drive in Racine and is open to the public when a conference is not in session. Call (262) 639–3211 to inquire.

Wake Up!
Sun Prairie

Jimmy the Groundhog lives on a small farm outside of Sun Prairie in a cement hutch with windows and a bed of hay. He has his own personal veterinarian and two groundhog keepers.

Once a year, early in the morning on February 2, a limousine pulls up outside Jimmy's little hutch and transports him in style to the Veterans of Foreign Wars parking lot in Sun Prairie. Television crews, reporters, city officials, and many others await his arrival. Will Jimmy cast a shadow when he emerges from the limo? If so, spring weather is more than six weeks away. If not, winter will end reasonably soon. (The seven generations of Jimmys—about fifty years' worth—claim better than 79 percent accuracy.)

By now it's only a few minutes after seven, Jimmy has gone home, and a thousand or so morning people are standing around in the cold. There's one more thing on the agenda, though: a big breakfast inside VFW Hall. There's also the Groundhog Ball, which is held the Saturday before Groundhog Day. Call (608) 837–4547 for details.

Wisconsin, birthplace of the blow dryer. Two companies that were developing electric blenders—Racine Universal Motor and Hamilton Beach of Two Rivers—were aware that women were using vacuum cleaners to dry their hair. They combined the technologies, and the first successful model was introduced in 1951. It had a nozzle attached to a pink plastic bonnet that fit over the head.

NOODLED UNTO DEATH
Watertown

Some years ago Watertown Goose was an impressive item on the menus of railroad dining cars and elegant restaurants in big cities. But how many fine lady and gentleman diners had a clue about what was going on in Watertown, Wisconsin?

Watertown geese were prized because they had been pampered, hand-fed, and *over*fed until they were hugely overweight, by about twenty pounds. (The geese had correspondingly large livers, which translated into pâté de foie gras.) This was accomplished by force-feeding them specially prepared noodles—big, fat multigrain noodles the size of sausages.

About four weeks before marketing time, a farmer schooled in the noodled-goose tradition began to make the rounds of his flock, holding each beak open with one hand and dropping the noodles down with the other. Each goose had to be fed several noodles every four or five hours around the clock. This meant that the entire family of a goose-noodler was involved, what with preparing special noodles (guess whose job that was?) and getting up at all hours of the night to noodle the geese.

Geese that got too fat to stand up anymore spent their last days in hammock contraptions. The largest Watertown goose ever shipped weighed 38½ pounds; the average was about 25. In one outstanding year 150,000 pounds of geese were shipped out of Watertown.

This famous local practice began in the 1880s and went on until twentieth-century federal meat-inspection laws forbade commercial butchering in the home—unless, of course, the goose-noodler's family hadn't already discovered that life had more to offer than this.

But the geese that gave their lives for the greater glory of Watertown have not been forgotten. For one thing, the Watertown High School athletic teams are still called the Goslings. For another, thanks to taxidermy, you can see a noodled goose, accompanied by livers (both noodled and normal), in Plank Road Barn behind Octagon House.

Octagon House, a popular Watertown landmark, is an eight-sided, fifty-seven-room brick house that was completed in 1854 as a family residence. On the grounds is the building where Margarethe Meyer Schurz began the first kindergarten in the United States, in 1856. Its interior depicts a class in session and displays some early teaching tools.

The historic buildings on the property are open to the public daily from May through October: 10:00 A.M. to 4:00 P.M. Memorial Day through Labor Day, 11:00 A.M. to 3:00 P.M. the rest of the time. Tours begin on the hour. Admission charge. For more information call (920) 261–2796.

This stuffed overstuffed goose can be seen in the barn behind Octagon House in Watertown, along with pale-red models of livers of a noodled goose (on the right) and a normal goose (left).

A WING AND A PRAYER
Waukesha

One fine morning in September 1941, flight instructor Dean Crites and his twenty-two-year-old student inspected their two-seater plane and took off from Milwaukee's Curtiss-Wright Airport (today Timmerman Field) for what was to be the student's graduation flight. They had just ascended to a thousand feet when suddenly there was a loud bang and a big jolt. The tail dropped, and the plane stalled and started in a loop. The student gladly turned the controls over to the instructor, who glided to a safe landing in an alfalfa field.

Not until they were on the ground did they discover that the entire engine had fallen out of the plane. (It was later pried out of Wisconsin Memorial Park cemetery, where it had been found buried a foot deep.) The very next day the brave lad went up again for his flight test.

The principal product of Van Holten, Inc., of Waterloo is a pickle in a pouch. After dealing in vinegar, pickles, and sauerkraut for forty years, in 1939 the company developed the idea and engineered the process of the individually packaged pickle. Today it is the only national distributor of such a thing. People who need a quick pickle hit buy thousands of them at truck stops, movie theaters, convenience stores, concession stands, and prisons. For a total pickle experience, they tip the plastic pouch and drink the brine.

A broken propeller blade on display at Waukesha County Airport represents all that is left of the plane today. Other exhibits tell the history of local aviation, from farm fields to jet landing strips. It began in 1912 with eighteen-year-old John Kaminski of Milwaukee, who performed exhibition flights in *Sweetheart,* a Curtiss Pusher biplane that had to be dismantled, shipped by train, and reassembled at the next air show. They tell more about Dean Crites, who could pick up a handkerchief with the wing tip of his WACO 10, and his brother Dale, pioneer aviators who built their first glider in 1919 and started the local flying school.

Mementos of simpler times include a pocket-size circle of plastic embossed with lines and numbers called a "Time-Speed Distance Computer," a slim pamphlet entitled "How to Fly a Piper Cub," aviation helmets, and Dale Crites's tan flight suit.

The exhibits are housed in the spiffy new terminal of Waukesha County Airport/Crites Field, 2525 Aviation Drive. More information is available by calling (262) 521–5249 or visiting the Web site at www.critesfield.com. From exit 294 off I–94, go south on County Highway J for 1 mile, then travel west on Northview Road for ½ mile, then north on Aviation Drive to the terminal.

A CLAIM TO FAME
PREVIOUSLY OVERLOOKED
Waukesha

Dave Kremer is the greatest stacker of bowling balls in the world. His unique skill began about ten years ago at a bowling alley. Just for his own entertainment—because, he says, he is not much of a bowler of bowling balls—he balanced one bowling ball on top of another ball and then a third on top of those two. There they stood. An onlooker was impressed. "Do it again and I'll pay you," he said, and became Dave's agent.

After practicing for several years in his garage in Waukesha, Dave earned a place in the *Guinness Book of World Records*—probably a permanent place, since he seems also to be the world's *only* bowling-ball stacker. His record is eleven balls. A challenger would need steady hands, good eyes, sturdy toes, a sense of humor, luck, an indulgent mate if any, and an appreciation for bowling-ball shape (bowling balls aren't perfectly round) and weight distribution.

Dave Kremer has to practice in the garage.

Dave Kremer has a real job and a wife and four young boys, and he doesn't stack bowling balls every day. But stacking them for fun has led to trips all over the world and to appearances on such TV shows as "Live with Regis and Kathie Lee" (Kathie kissed him on the head) and "Ripley's Believe It or Not." He is also the December page in Guinness's year 2000 calendar.

TURKEY GEHRKE, THE HUMAN HIBERNATOR

Arthur Gehrke, better known around Watertown as "Turkey," hibernated like a bear every winter. He crawled under the covers in the middle of November and emerged in the spring, about the time baseball practice started (he was, of course, a Cubs fan).

Newspapers picked up the story. Ripley's Believe It or Not radio show played him up. A London haberdashery sent silk pajamas. A Milwaukee psychiatrist visited and diagnosed "a typical case of mixed compulsion and anxiety neurosis." For whatever reason, the cramps and pains Gehrke suffered every November went away if he went to bed and stayed there, so that's just what he did.

Turkey Gehrke died in his sleep in January 1942 at age fifty-nine, partway into his thirtieth winter of hibernating.

WHERE THE WILDERNESS
MEETS CONGO BONGO
Wisconsin Dells

Where to begin? The Dells—the Midwest's most popular family vacation spot, one of America's most amazing tourism meccas—offers an embarrassment of riches.

There's Air Boingo Bungee Jump, Extreme World, Count Wolff Von Baldasar's Haunted Mansion, and Mass Panic. Noah's Ark, America's largest indoor water park, has thirty-two water-slides, 5,000 inner tubes, and such options for getting wet as Congo Bongo Rapids, Kowabunga, and Flash Flood.

With places like Serpent Safari, Laser Storm, and about eighty other major attractions to choose from, it's no wonder many people who come to the Dells stay for days without ever seeing the dells—the part that began millions of years BTB (Before Tommy Bartlett). In relative peace and quiet, guides on boat tours point out beautiful, unique rock formations along the Wisconsin River: Cow in the Milk Bottle, Devil's Elbow, Baby Grand Piano, Hawk's Bill. Some of the boats are ducks, modified World War II amphibious vehicles.

The name "Tommy Bartlett" means water skiing, bumper stickers, and the presence of a Russian MIR space station at the Dells. In the 1950s Bartlett started the Thrill Show on Water, which inspired other spectacles and remains a classic. The Dells wasn't just for fishing anymore.

The Dells occupies about 20 square miles of the communities of Wisconsin Dells and Lake Delton to the east of I–90/94. Outdoor attractions are open Memorial Day through Labor Day. Many indoor attractions are open year-round. All charge admission. Details at www.wisdells.com.

Warming up at Tommy Bartlett's
Thrill Show. What next? The incredible trapeze toe-hang?

*T*ommy Bartlett entered show business at age thirteen on radio station *WISN* in his hometown of Milwaukee. By the time he was twenty, he was announcing as many as seven soap operas a day in Chicago. His fame grew as host of "Meet the Missus" and "Welcome Travelers."

*T*HE *W*ONDER *S*POT
Wisconsin Dells

The gravity-defying Wonder Spot is in a class by itself, and not only because it's located in a pretty wooded setting just off the main drag. Water flows upward, chairs balance on two legs, people lean at weird angles. Everything is a bit off kilter, as it has been since someone built a cabin here in 1948 and abandoned it because he said a mysterious force made him unable to walk, pour, or see straight when he lived here. Visitors agree it's a goofy place.

From Highway 12 turn in at R Place Restaurant (444 Wisconsin Dells Parkway South), and follow the road around back to the Wonder Spot. Open daily 9:00 A.M. to 9:00 P.M. in the summer. Admission charge. Call (608) 254–4224 for more information.

SOUTHWEST

SOMETHING OUT OF NOTHING
Baraboo

Several metal creatures alongside the highway and a simple DELANEY'S SURPLUS sign identify Dr. Evermor's location, but they hardly prepare you for what lies behind the trees and down the driveway. It's a fantastic garden of scrap metal, now assembled into giant insectoids and birds; a philharmonic-size bird orchestra; and the 250-ton Forevertron, the world's largest scrap-metal sculpture, according to the *Guinness Book of World Records.*

Dr. Evermor's Forevertron,
the world's largest scrap-metal sculpture.

Early in the 1940s, when he was little Tom Every growing up in Brooklyn, Wisconsin, Dr. Evermor was flattening tin cans and toothpaste tubes and saving foil from gum wrappers for the war effort, along with everyone else. With this early conditioning in recycling, he grew up to run an industrial salvage business and to appreciate what industrial designers could do with iron, steel, brass, bronze, and copper. He also developed a fine collection of dynamos, survey markers, sheet metal, springs, pipes, chains, chimes, wrenches, musical instruments, blades, cables, the decontamination chamber from the Apollo space mission, and much, much more. With these materials he creates gigantic yet intricate sculptures.

He believes deeply in making something out of nothing. "That is exactly what Dr. Evermor is all about," he says.

Dr. Evermor is a self-taught artist who uses no blueprints, no sketches, nothing. He doesn't even think about it—"I just go for it." His work attracts television crews, filmmakers, artists, inventors, children, and a great assortment of humanity.

Someday, Dr. Evermor hopes, all this will be displayed across the highway at the former Badger Army Munitions Plant as a historic museum of industrial design and a memorial to wartime munitions workers and to farm families who had to give up their land to make room for the plant. Until that occurs, Dr. Evermor's Art Park is on the west side of Highway 12, just north of County Highway C, and 7 miles south of the Baraboo city limits. Consistent with the creator's spirit, there are no tours, no admission fee, no signs to explain anything. But there might be Dr. Evermor—he's often on site—in pith helmet with cigar.

FLAP YOUR ELBOWS, SPIN YOUR EARS, AND FLY AWAY
Baraboo

The International Crane Foundation has every species of crane in the world—and George Archibald. He too is a tall and rare bird. "I'd do almost anything for a crane!" says Archibald, director of ICF.

Archibald's earliest childhood memory is of being two years old and crawling after a mother duck and her ducklings. When he got older his parents let him raise chickens, ducks, pheasants, turkeys, and even peacocks. By the time he was out of college, he was dancing around like a crane to encourage female cranes to lay eggs, and dressing up like a crane to take care of young birds.

It's all very scientific, as he has explained to audiences far and wide; a newborn crane thinks that the first large moving thing it sees is its mother, so it's important to establish the crane image from the start. Endangered cranes all over the world were in big trouble before Archibald and others at ICF came to their rescue, and they're all breathing easier now.

The International Crane Foundation is the only place in the world where you can see all fifteen of the world's crane species, including the sarus crane, at 6 feet easily the tallest flying bird in the world. You might also see some staff "chick parents" dressed like cranes. From chick parents baby cranes learn where to find food, how to go to water, and to be alert.

ICF is about 5 miles north of Baraboo and 1 mile east of Highway 12 on Shady Lane Road. Hours are from 9:00 A.M. to 5:00 P.M. daily, May 1 through October 31. Admission charge. For information about cranes, special events, and tours, see the ICF's Web site at www.savingcranes.org or call (608) 356–9462.

A chick parent at the International Crane Foundation wears

a crane costume so that the birds don't get too attached to humans.

C I R C U S   W O R L D   M U S E U M
B a r a b o o

Baraboo is the only place in Wisconsin where elephants splash in the river in summertime. They're taking a break before it's back to work at the Big Top Show at the Circus World Museum.

The year-round exhibit hall has such novel sights as the sparkly little wedding clothes of "the smallest man in the world," 33-inch Michu, and his bride, Julianna, also a midget but several inches taller. Though never husband and wife, they recited marriage vows twice a day throughout 1976 and 1977 in mock ceremonies before thousands of witnesses, reenacting the storied wedding of Tom Thumb and his bride in 1863. The chair that Clyde Beatty used in his wild-animal act is here, too. It's an ordinary kitchen chair with one leg missing (gnawed off?). You can also learn about the canvas tutus worn by elephants that performed in an original Balanchine–Stravinsky ballet and about the night in 1885 when a speeding train plowed into Jumbo the elephant. Posters tell of intrepid, intricate feats on a single strand of wire at dizzying heights.

It's all here because Baraboo was home until about 1918 to the Ringling Brothers, "The World's Greatest Showmen" (they started out with a small tent, three horses, and a hyena), and to their circus as well.

Located at 426 Water Street (Highway 113). Circus performances daily from early May through Labor Day. Exhibit hall, circus-wagon pavilion, and wagon-restoration center open daily year-round except major holidays. Admission charge. For twenty-four-hour information call (608) 356–0800; office (608) 356–8341; www.circusworldmuseum.com.

WISCONSIN DEATH TRAP
Black River Falls

The current report on Black River Falls snowmobile trails is, due to a lack of snow this La Niña winter, "the corners are a little rough." In an ordinary winter the Falls is an outdoor paradise for snowmobilers, cross-country skiers, dogsledders, and snowboarders. Once it warms, the Black River and the state forest surrounding the handsome little community provide virtually every kind of outdoor experience you could hope for. As the Chamber of Commerce likes to say, "Nowhere in this great continent of ours can be found a more desirable residence."

It's just that, for a few years back in the 1890s, everyone in Black River Falls seemed to go crazy. Michael Lesy captured it in *Wisconsin Death Trip* (1973), a pastiche of mortuary photographs, newspaper clippings, and admissions records of the Mendota Mental Asylum culled from the *Badger State Banner*, a tabloid published in Black River Falls by Frank and George Cooper that leaned heavily toward human interest and misery.

For whatever reasons—economic or personal depression, disease, crop failure, just plain loneliness (some have even cited "ethnic tendencies of the Scandinavian and German populations")—all manner of weird goings-on went on. Windows were smashed, children ran wild, fires were set, farmers used dynamite for pillows, and chickens were decapitated in bizarre rituals, all recorded by photographer Charles Van Schaick, whose studios now house the Jackson County Historical Society (where the number-one attraction is his "Wisconsin Death Trip" collection).

It could be that this sort of thing went on in isolated rural areas everywhere in the Midwest, but there was just no Van Schaick to record it. *Wisconsin Death Trip* is now a cottage industry in Black River Falls and is even sold on the town's official Web site, www.blackriverfalls.com. A recent film by James Marsh can only stir the pot. The Charles Van Schaick Photo Gallery is at 13 South First Street, Black River Falls, and houses many of the photographs seen in "Death Trip." Open by appointment only. Call (715) 284–5314.

2001: A BEER ODYSSEY
Black River Falls

Construction is under way for a 138-foot beer stein. It is scheduled for completion in 2001; this being Wisconsin, it will probably be tipped back and emptied early in 2002. Essentially a stein-shaped mall, it will house retail and gift shops, as well as a few offices and a museum or two. The lid of the stein will enclose a Renaissance-style restaurant and pub, and the dual glass elevators in the handle will offer a panoramic view of the countryside.

The ten-story stein will be located at I–94 and Highway 54 (exit 116), not far from the enormous orange

Coming soon to Black River Falls, the world's largest beer stein.

moose that has long been a familiar landmark. Call Susan
Sampson of Sampson Art Galleries in Black River Falls
for more information: (800) 253–3271 or (715) 284–5223.

THOU SHALT NOT
STEAL THE TOILETRIES
Boscobel

Janesville salesman John "Nick" Nicholson had had a hard
day on the road when he checked in to the Boscobel Hotel,
or "Central House," as it was known in 1898. He was not
pleased (1) to learn that no single rooms were available, and (2)
to find the hotel "crowded with drummers and hang-abouts
playing cards, shaking dice, smoking, laughing, cursing,
yelling and singing with clinking of glasses and men drunk
and asleep in chairs." He was, however, willing to share a double room (Room 19) with, as it turned out, a kindred spirit,
Beloit salesman Sam Hill.

Nicholson and Hill agreed that "Christian traveling men"
needed suitable ways to pass the time, so they organized what
eventually became the Gideons International Society. Today the
Gideons make sure that hotel rooms all over the world contain
Bibles—that's about 45 million Bibles per year, or eighty-six
nightstand drawers per minute.

Senator John F. Kennedy and his wife, Jacqueline, occupied
Room 19 for a few hours on the afternoon of March 25, 1960,
and then had dinner. JFK was campaigning for the Democratic
nomination for president, and the Wisconsin primary was coming up. It is not known how much of that time they spent on
Bible study.

The local historical society has outfitted Room 19 in period
furniture, and you can ask to see it by calling (608) 375–4714.

The 1863 building isn't functioning as a hotel now, but it has a restaurant and bar, as well as a lobby that displays Gideon Bibles in several languages. It is located on Wisconsin Avenue in downtown Boscobel.

AND ON THE SEVENTH DAY THE WEGNERS RESTED
Cataract

Before the era of television and professional football, families piled into the car and went out for Sunday drives. In this part of Wisconsin, one of the places they headed for, if not over, was Cataract.

The big attraction was the concrete-and-glass creations of Paul and Matilda Wegner. Cars lined up for miles to see the church, the steamship, the anniversary cake, an American flag—thirty sculptures in all. A peace monument even became a "speakers' corner" for preachers and politicians.

The Wegners created all of this during their retirement. They were German immigrants who first farmed and later ran the Ford dealership in the nearby town of Bangor. (They raised five children along the way.) Then one day in 1929, they ventured south to Dickeyville and beheld Father Wernerus's grotto (page 191). After that experience, sculptures and structures with themes of patriotism, religion, and travel began taking shape on their own property.

The Wegners taught themselves to become skilled architects and designers specializing in intricate mosaics. The profusely embellished exterior of the glass church has views of eleven different churches; the interior has equally intricate ecumenical references. It was the scene of many weddings as well as Paul Wegner's funeral. The steamship represents the *Bremen*,

*This 12-foot fiberglass mouse is
named for the great Russian composer Igor Stravinsky,
who died on the day that Igor arrived in Fennimore, April 6, 1971.
He stands in front of Fennimore Cheese on Highway 61 on the south
side of Fennimore.*

which brought the Wegners to this country in 1886, and the giant wedding cake honors their fifty-two years together.

The Kohler Foundation funded restoration of the site and deeded the Paul and Matilda Wegner Grotto to Monroe County, which maintains it as an outdoor museum and public park. Located on Highway 71, 9.2 miles north of Sparta or 1.5 miles south of Cataract, it is open year-round. For information call the Monroe County Local History Room at (608) 269–8680.

ONE CURE FOR OLD-AGE BOREDOM
Cochrane

Herman Rusch was another energetic, self-taught, late-blooming artist who emerged in the 1950s. At age seventy-one he discovered his medium to be glass-and-cement. He proceeded to spread his whimsical dinosaurs, flamingos, polar bears, snakes, and a Hindu temple over several acres of land south of Cochrane, near the Mississippi River. He also surrounded them with ornamental spires and gates and enclosed them in a spectacular, 260-foot-long arching fence. "You could go around the world five times and never see another like it," he said.

Rusch's work has won high praise for its sense of design and wit, but Herman seemed not to have taken himself too seriously. According to the inscription on a bust of himself, creating this wondrous world was just "a good way to kill old-age boredom." He died in 1985, eleven days after his one hundredth birthday, having successfully lived up to his claim that "a fellow should leave a few tracks."

Herman's "tracks" were recently restored by the Kohler Foundation and donated to the Town of Milton. To reach Prairie Moon Sculpture Garden and Museum take Highway 35 northwest from Fountain City about 6 miles; just past the

IF YOUR NAME IS CUBA CITY, YOU TRY HARDER

Cuba City has a salute to U.S. presidents all up and down Main Street. It started in 1976 as a bicentennial project and ended up turning Cuba City into the "City of Presidents."

Every president has his name and profile on a red-white-and-blue shield attached to a lamppost. Presidents are paired chronologically on back-to-back shields, starting with Washington and Adams at the corner of North Main and Benton. They proceed down Main Street (Fillmore and Pierce are outside the Owl Furniture Store, for instance) to the First Methodist Church (Arthur and Cleveland), then hop across the street and head north again (Truman and Ike land outside Hindu's Corner Bar, and Nixon and Ford are by Antiques Unlimited). Police and librarians at the municipal building keep an eye on Bush and Clinton outside their door.

Cuba City was originally named Yuba, but confusion with another Yuba in Wisconsin (two Yubas?) led to renaming it Cuba, and then Cuba City. It's on Highway 80, just a few miles north of the Illinois border.

Cochrane-Fountain City School, turn left onto Prairie Moon Road; the site is located half a mile farther, on the left. The garden is open year-round, dawn to dusk. The museum is open 1:00 to 4:00 P.M. Saturday and Sunday, May through September. Call (608) 687–9874 for more information.

HOLY GHOST PARK
Dickeyville

In both mass and message, the Dickeyville Grotto is the weightiest of Wisconsin's cement parks. No whimsical creatures cavort here. Instead there are awesome altars and shrines labeled with straightforward commands—FAITH, PEACE, CHASTITY, MILDNESS, LONG SUFFERING, PATIENCE, FORTITUDE— and encrusted with glassware, pottery, fossils, Indian relics, and hornets' nests.

This is the work of Father Mathias Wernerus, who, in the 1920s, saw it as "God's wonderful

One of the "Religion in Stone" areas at Holy Ghost Park at Dickeyville.

material collected from all parts of the world. . . . Future generations will still enjoy the fruit of our labor and will bless the
man that conceived and built this thing." He was right. Each
year about 60,000 people view the altars, shrines, fountains,
gardens, and sculptures on the grounds of Holy Ghost Parish.

Father Wernerus, a missionary priest who grew up among
outdoor shrines in Germany, had a lot of assistance from
parishioners and schoolchildren. They hauled rocks and concrete, contributed materials from home, and helped with decoration and construction. The Dickeyville Grotto is actually a
collaborative project representing the geology of the upper Mississippi region, the religious and patriotic beliefs of Father
Wernerus and his parishioners, and the crockery and figurines
of their combined households.

The Grotto is on Highway 61 just north of Dickeyville.
Grounds open year-round. Tours daily between 11:00 A.M. and
4:00 P.M. June through August. Gift shop open daily 9:00 A.M.
to 6:00 P.M., from April through October. Call (608) 568–3119
for details.

Is That a Stratocruiser or Are You Just Happy to See Me?
Dodgeville

A few miles south of House on the Rock (page 217), while
your head is still spinning, you come upon a Boeing C-97
Stratocruiser parked alongside Highway 23. It's the size of half
a football field, and during the Korean War it transported
troops and cargo.

It's a landmark for the Don Q Inn, which lies just beyond.
The elaborate plans that Don Quinn, who owned the hotel then,
had in mind for the plane didn't quite work out, but other ideas
have. The Dodgeville train station was moved here and con-

verted to sleeping rooms, the steeple from an 1850s Methodist church became a honeymoon suite, copper cheese vats were converted to bathtubs, and barber chairs from shops in Fennimore and an Iowa penitentiary offer seating in the lobby.

It isn't exactly the plane and local history that bring many people here, however. The Don Q has fantasy suites that offer travelers an opportunity to bed down in an igloo, a space capsule, a thatched jungle hut, and a hot-air balloon, among other novel accommodations.

All this and a restaurant, too. Highway 23 North. Call (608) 935–2321 for information.

A Stratocruiser

helps to locate the Don Q Inn.

NOT HOUSE ON THE ROCK, BUT ROCK IN THE HOUSE
Fountain City

At 11:38 A.M. on April 24, 1995, Maxine Anderson was admiring her newly decorated bedroom—the wallpaper with its tiny blue flowers and border of cabbage roses, the full-length mirrors on the closet doors—when she heard a noise that was worse than thunder. She headed for the door, and seconds later a fifty-five-ton boulder landed where she had been standing. For thousands of years it had hovered high up on the bluff behind the house. (Today you can look up and see the gap, like a missing tooth, in a row of boulders like this one.)

The Andersons promptly moved out and sold the house as is, rock, debris, and all, to people with an eye for its tourism possibilities.

Strangely enough, the same thing happened to a house next door in April 1901. This runaway

This is not the look the Andersons had in mind for the master bedroom.

rock, however, killed a Mrs. Dubler as she slept. Her husband awoke to find himself in the cellar amid the ruins of their home. A garage stands on the site now.

Fountain City has antiques stores, art galleries, and a timeless look. Rock in the House is located toward the north end of town and faces the Mississippi River, at 440 North Shore Drive (Highway 35, the Great River Road). Open—is it ever—daily from 10:00 A.M. to 5:00 P.M., year-round.

S E R E N D I P I T Y   I N   H A R D W A R E
G e n o a

The words "Ohmigosh, I've been looking for this for years" ring out at Old Tool Shed Antiques. Gayhart Swenson and his son Rick lovingly rescue, clean, repair, display, and sell old hand tools. Handmade tools are especially admired here, from the simple plumb bobs that boys made in high school shop class to very complex contraptions. In addition to hundreds of hammers, chisels, and drills are the more offbeat fire-hose nozzles (Gay and Rick are both retired firefighters), rope winders, ornate cast-iron tractor seats, goose-wing axes, denture makers, cigar-box openers, and much more that you'll never see at Home Depot.

Some items at Old Tool Shed Antiques are so old that hardly anyone knows what they ever were used for. *Hardly* anyone, because it's really a matter of waiting for the right person to come through the door. Not long ago a mystery tool sat on the front counter for several months until at last a stranger entered the shop and with one glance announced, "I know what that is, and I have the instruction booklet at home." On his next visit, instructions and Mend-a-Rip (a hand-sewing device that cowboys carried to repair saddles and chaps) were reunited.

You might want to celebrate finding that wrench that completes your set over a platter of catfish cheeks at one of the local restaurants. Genoa (pronounced "GeNOa," despite its Italian heritage) is on the Mississippi River, 17 miles south of La Crosse on Highway 35 (the Great River Road). Old Tool Shed Antiques occupies an 1867 building at 612 Main Street. Open 10:00 A.M. to 5:00 P.M. Thursday through Monday, or by chance or appointment. Call (608) 689–2066.

Eat Your Heart Out, Claes Oldenburg
Gotham

In February 1999 a winter ice storm damaged a tall conifer in a small grove of Norwegian spruces at the Merry Farm of Gotham. When the broken branches were cleared away, the owners saw that the forces of Nature had selected their property as the site of a modern icon: a felt-tip marker, 9 feet tall. They commissioned a wood sculptor to smooth out the contours and added a bronze plaque declaring it a historical marker.

The marker stands between a brown house and a brown barn in a small grove of tall pine trees. The owners are friendly. The property has beautiful gardens and has been the scene of weddings (instead of saying "I will," one bride said, "If you change your attitude, I will"), barn dances, and folk concerts. Take Highway 14 to Gotham; go east on County Highway JJ for ¾ mile and north on Moss Hollow for 1 mile; at the sharp turn right, go straight to the end of Slow Lane to number 30999.

The historical felt-tip marker at

Merry Farm of Gotham, sculpture by Michael Feeney.

THE EIGHT-LEGGED PIG IS JUST ICING ON THE CAKE
Hatfield

The Thunderbird Museum, located in a clearing in the forest in Hatfield, is bursting with the collections of Violet Teeples and her neighbors. Teeples was an amateur anthropologist and archeologist, as well as a beachcomber, artist, lecturer, and businesswoman. Before opening the Thunderbird she owned several businesses in Hatfield: the Roller Rink and Bar, the Hatfield Grocery Store and Bar, and an antiques shop.

The Thunderbird Museum reflects her lifelong study of Indians, particularly the tribes of Jackson County, and her hobby of collecting Indian artifacts (she found her first arrowhead when she was three). When the museum opened in 1961, Winnebagoes in full regalia performed tribal music and dances.

Violet Teeples intended the Thunderbird to be an Indian museum, but her neighbors started giving her so many of their own treasures that it is a mélange instead. Their generosity accounts for the presence of a six-legged frog, an eight-legged pig, a dentist's chair in which a man was stabbed to death in 1904, a 10-foot hand-carved fireplace from France, and much more. Among the rare Indian artifacts are primitive spears, bows and arrows from all over the world, zillions of arrowheads and weapons, dioramas of Indian life that Teeples made herself, an original translation of the Winnebago Bible, and a photograph of John F. Kennedy in a feathered headdress with Winnebago chief Alvin Blackdeer.

There's loads of everything, enough to fill twenty-one rooms of what was once the old Hatfield Hotel. If you can't find something here you like, chances are you don't like anything.

Follow the signs from Highway E in Hatfield to N9517 Thunderbird Lane. Open 9:00 A.M. to 5:00 P.M. daily, Memorial Day through Labor Day. Admission charge. Call (715) 333–5841 for more information.

A R T   F O R   N I C K ' S   S A K E
H o l l a n d a l e

Nicholas Engelbert was different from other dairy farmers. He read a book while walking his cows along the highway to graze (he owned only fourteen acres). And on the lawn of his farmhouse were all these creations that he put together when he got home: Paul Bunyan, Uncle Sam, Snow White and the Seven Dwarfs, Vikings, lions, elephants, eagles, peacocks. He used metal parts from around the barnyard, stones from the stream, glass and china from the kitchen, and concrete for glue. As if Nick had a lot of glass-and-concrete batter left over one day, the exterior of his two-story house acquired a façade to match the sculpture.

The Engelbert place eventually became quite a roadside attraction, so Nick provided a parking lot and picnic grounds for visitors. Every year his wife planted flowers that spelled out PEACE.

But Nick died on his eighty-first birthday in 1962, and his artwork fell into disrepair. Pieces disappeared, though the mailman tried to keep an eye on things. In 1991 the Kohler Foundation came to the rescue. It restored many pieces and turned the project over to the Pecatonia Foundation, which operates Grandview as a historic folk-art site. The house is open, and Nick's paintings of family life hang on the walls.

Grandview is located on the south side of Highway 39 just west of Hollandale. The museum is open daily 9:00 A.M. to

5:00 P.M. from Memorial Day through Labor Day or at other times by arrangement; the grounds are sometimes open longer. If the gate is open, go in. Call (608) 967–2322 or 967–2140 for more information.

Nick Engelbert depicted his family in this family tree. He and his wife are on the lower branches, their children are playing and doing hobbies they liked, and the fellow at the bottom is one of the tramps who enjoyed the Engelberts' hospitality over the years.

POP-BOTTLE GARDEN
La Crosse

Paul Hefti's primary media are stuffed animals and green plastic soft-drink bottles (if he needs red or white, he'll saw off the bottom, paint the insides, and re-assemble). His accent pieces are ice-cream cartons, lamp bases, toys, plastic flowers, and fans. His creations fill a large fenced-in corner lot, about 60 by 90 feet. Some are anchored to the ground, and some hang from trees.

Holiday greetings from Paul Hefti, 1999.

Some are complex: The "It's Milk" sculpture is a Rube Gold-berg–style arrangement of bottles and tubes. Some are simple: A pale-yellow plastic locomotive perches on a pole to which a small bald doll is pinned by her hula hoop. A frilly lampshade tops off a plastic wishing well.

Alongside the house are small special-event shrines where bottles observe the season or spell out HAPPY BIRTHDAY TO YOU. Walk up to the LOOK IN GLASS and discover one of the puns that Paul Hefti is known for. He is in his eighties and lives in the small red brick house next door.

It's obvious that a lot of thought has gone into the work, and although no single theme comes through, the overall effect is colorful and upbeat. Despite the severe La Crosse winters that they must endure, the large population of somewhat-the-worse-for-wear pandas, bunnies, bears, reindeer, and duckies constantly smile back at visitors to this jolly environment.

It is located at Fifth Avenue and Adams, just east of the curve in Highway 14 as it heads toward downtown La Crosse.

Black squirrels abound in Norwalk, and, about 80 miles to the east, albino squirrels thrive in the subdivisions on the north shore of Lake Puckaway.

VALLEY OF THE DOLLS
La Crosse

If there's a doll in your past, no matter when, look here long enough and you're sure to see a familiar face. How could anyone be missing? The La Crosse Doll Museum has about 7,200 dolls on display, from early bisque to Jesse Ventura.

In addition to the mainstream favorites, there are child-star dolls (such as Deanna Durbin, Shirley Temple, and Buffy), advertising dolls (icons of Oscar Mayer, Tidy Cat, Morton Salt, Bubble Yum); and public figures (JFK and Jackie, Margaret Thatcher, and Abe Lincoln). There are baby dolls (one resembles Humphrey Bogart—he did, after all, pose for Gerber baby-food labels) and "less than pretty" dolls (including an Amy that escaped Rosalynn's bonfire on the White House lawn). And if you think your Crissy With Hair That Grows and Grows and Grows was a first, a 1920s doll with a lever that moves her horse hair up and down shows that Crissy was not.

A display case 82 feet long contains the largest collection of Barbies in the Northern Hemisphere and in action. Barbie makes toast in her dream kitchen, she steps out with Dance Magic Ken, she paddles past her beach house. Each Barbie is displayed with her original outfits and accessories, in case you no longer remember the earrings that got lost the first day or the rightful owner of the white go-go boots.

Darlene Mueller, collector and curator, knows stories behind them all, and she sometimes dresses like Raggedy Ann for group tours. Her museum at 1213 Caledonia Street, in Old Towne North, is open 10:00 A.M. to 5:00 P.M. Monday through Saturday, 11:00 A.M. to 4:30 P.M. Sunday. Admission charge. Call (608) 785–0020 for more details.

ONE BIG M
Platteville

The 241-foot letter M that overlooks Grant County from a mound east of Platteville is the work of energetic and competitive students of the Wisconsin Mining School, circa the late 1930s. Other mining schools had big M's, but the Wisconsin boys made sure that they hauled enough limestone to make their school's the biggest.

The M is lighted at night on two annual occasions: University of Wisconsin–Platteville homecoming in the fall, and the "M" Ball in the spring. Members of a coed professional engineering fraternity accomplish this by placing about 500 coffee cans around the outside of the M. Inside each can is a smaller can, with a few rocks between the two for ballast. Kerosene and a particle-board wick go into each smaller can. Theta Taus dash around with road flares lighting the wicks, and the M burns for about forty-five minutes.

In 1998 a member of the Platteville Jaycees had a brilliant idea. He rounded up about 250 Plattevillians who were willing to dress in black (black trash bags, if necessary), trudge up the 260 steps, and arrange themselves in the shape of mouse ears in the V part of the M. An aerial photographer snapped the scene, and the photo won for Platteville the grand prize in a nationwide contest sponsored by Disney: Mickey's Hometown Parade. On July Fourth about 50,000 people (many in mouse ears) lined Main Street to see such sights as thirty Disney floats; the Cuba City High School band in Pluto hats; and Mickey, Minnie, and Donald, waving and bowing. That night $100,000 worth of fireworks went off at the world's biggest M.

The M is about 4 miles northeast of Platteville on County Highway B. Students from the College of Engineering, Mathematics and Science maintain the M.

*More than 260
steps lead to the
top of the big M,
but once there
you'd have to be
about 20 feet tall
to view the
world's largest W. You can, however,
survey the countryside for miles around or zoom in on tiny cows with the
telescope provided here (free—no quarters necessary).*

DR. BEAUMONT'S DIET PLAN
Prairie du Chien

The exhibits on early medicine at the Prairie du Chien Museum at Fort Crawford are enough to make you shudder. Especially "Doctors on Horseback" from the 1840s. You'd have to be in pretty bad shape to be glad to see one of these guys coming up the driveway. In his saddlebags might be a pocket surgical kit of handmade instruments, a lancet or "scarificator" for bleeding, a turnkey for extracting teeth. But the price was right. In 1846 the bill for one patient came to only $46, including $10 for "amputating all the toes of one foot." Doc's snowshoes and lantern complete the picture in this exhibit.

Apparently things improved slightly later on. There were dentists with offices (and foot-operated drills) and horse-and-buggy doctors with manufactured, though still scary-looking, instruments that came in nice lined cases.

It was at Fort Crawford that Dr. William Beaumont conducted experiments on the hapless Alexis St. Martin, a voyageur who had suffered a gunshot wound to his left side that left a hole after it healed. Dr. Beaumont found it absolutely fascinating to tie bits of food to a string, drop them into the hole, then pull them out to see the effect of Alexis's stomach juices. This went on for several years of co-dependence, after which, in 1833, Dr. Beaumont published the book that

A diorama at the Fort Crawford medical
museum depicts an amputation on a patient who appears to have
passed out. Anesthesia didn't come along until 1846. Medicine was more
casual then—doctors in street clothes, leg in bucket, surgical saw on floor.

explained the physiology of digestion once and for all. His work is recognized here, along with other milestones in medicine. Dioramas show foot-tall medical professionals calmly removing tumors and amputating limbs, the patients' little faces contorted in agony, until, at last, *anesthesia!* in 1846.

In a lighter vein, a forthcoming exhibit will feature medical quackery, such as helmets to make hair grow and ray guns to cure whatever ails you.

The Prairie du Chien Museum at Fort Crawford, 717 South Beaumont Road, is open daily 10:00 A.M. to 5:00 P.M. from May 1 through October 31. Admission charge. Call (608) 326–6960 for more information.

REAL TOUGH LOVE
Prairie du Chien

Beneath the Crawford County Courthouse lies an unusual slice of territorial history: a jail that was built in 1843, though it could better be described as a dungeon.

The five largest cells measure only 5 by 7 feet. Each has a tiny window (wriggle out? no way!) and a bunk bed. Yes, *two* sorry souls shared this space no bigger than a bus shelter. Two cells are only 3 feet wide and have no bed—temporary holding cells, we have to hope. For the most miserable wretches, there was solitary confinement in two cells barely high enough to stand in, no window at all, and equipped with leg irons and arm chains. Something like a *Far Side* cartoon.

It's enough to make you watch your step around the courthouse. NO SMOKING. DON'T LITTER. Whatever you say, sir. Of course, the jail hasn't been in use since 1896, when a new one was built.

If you'd like to see the territorial jail, call the Crawford County clerk at (608) 326–0200 to arrange a tour. Recently the county replaced the original rubble floors with concrete to ensure safe footing for visitors.

MEADOW MUFFINS
Prairie du Sac

To the officials of the Wisconsin State Cow Chip Throw, the competitive tossing of dried cow manure would seem to be a serious matter: Contestants must select their chips from the wagonload provided by the Official Meadow Muffin Committee. Only two chips per contestant. Chips shall be at least 6 inches in diameter. No gloves. After all, a trip to the national championship in Beaver, Oklahoma, is at stake.

In 1999 an Oak Creek woman continued her ten-year reign as top woman tosser, scoring a distance of 137 feet 6 inches. Other annual events include the Tournament of Chips Parade, "the world's only cow pie eating contest," bovine bingo (a wandering cow lets the chips fall where they may on a numbered grid), 5K and 10K runs, jugglers and magicians, arts and crafts, music and dancing, food and beer.

The event is held during the first weekend in September. Follow the signs off business Highway 12 (Water Street) to Marion Park. Call (608) 643–4317 to inquire and register to throw.

*Ammunition for the Cow
Chip Throw, and more where those came from. The meadow
muffins are collected from cow pastures by community-spirited
volunteers, then sun-dried.*

WE WILL WE WILL ROCKWELL
Reedsburg

Norman Rockwell's hometown museum in Stockbridge, Massachusetts, has original oil paintings. "Norman Rockwell: Pictures for the American People," the current traveling retrospective, consists of oils and the 322 *Saturday Evening Post* covers. But the Museum of Norman Rockwell Art in downtown Reedsburg has about eight times as much to show for the artist's total output. They are reproductions, but so were the *Post* covers, which were plenty good enough for millions of readers for almost fifty years. Here are not only all 322 covers but also about 4,000 other examples of his work.

The Reedsburg museum shows the vast scope of Rockwell's career by including all the published pieces—covers, calendars, story illustrations, and advertisements for Jell-O, McDonald's, Crest, Goodyear, Lifebuoy, Niblets. We see ordinary Americans doing ordinary things, reassuring and sentimental scenes of Granddad carving the Thanksgiving turkey, Sonny in the barber chair, Sis and Bobby at the soda fountain after the prom.

Rockwell may never have set foot here, but his work seems quite at home in Reedsburg. Museum of Norman Rockwell Art, 227 South Park Street. Open daily 9:00 A.M. to 5:00 P.M. from mid-May to mid-October; winter hours vary. Admission charge. Call (608) 524–2123 for more information.

*City Brewery, the new owner
of the old Old Style brewery in La Crosse,
plans to give the world's largest six-pack a new look.*

A TWO-WAY PARADE
Retreat

A two-way parade—one that proceeds to the end of the parade route, turns around, and comes back—is extremely rare, but it's a regular feature of the annual fair in the rural community of Retreat. Parade units represent the Retreat Ramblers 4-H Club, a veterinarian, fertilizer and feed companies, volunteer fire departments, and a church or two. A small junior high school band leads the way.

The parade starts at the old cheese factory and doubles back at the feed store. Radio station WBRQ is there to provide live coverage.

Retreat has a population of fewer than a hundred and consists of only a church, a community building, a pole shed, a cemetery, a small agri-business, and a small grade school. Yet hundreds of people from all over come to the fair (sometimes called the Retreat World's Fair), which started in 1919. A talent show on the wooden stage of the 1928 community building follows the parade, and a horse show goes on all day. That night a dance ends the fair.

Retreat is on County Highway N in the southwest corner of Vernon County, and the fair is held in late September or early October. Call the Retreat Sportsmen's Club for more information at (608) 648–3493.

LAW OF GRAVITY REPEALED
Shullsburg

A short length of pavement on County Highway U south of Shullsburg is known far and wide as Gravity Hill. Farmers are used to seeing folks from all over creation out here on this little two-lane road, bean fields on both sides, lurching around as they stop their cars, back up, turn around, and try it again. The big attraction is the eerie sensation that occurs when your eyes say you're going downhill but your car says you're going uphill.

For the thrill of Gravity Hill, stop right here and shift into neutral.

To try it, start from the Shullsburg water tower. Your destination is only about 1 mile south. After you pass Rennick Road
on your left (at about 0.8 miles) and are heading downhill, look
for a yellow, diamond-shaped sign with a black arrow and a 25
mph sign below. About three fourths of the way to the bottom
of this hill but before you get to the sign, stop, put the car in
neutral, and feel it roll—uphill. The phenomenon defies an easy
explanation.

MINER
TRANSGESSIONS

*Highway U is also known as Judgement Street.
That and other street names in Shullsburg (such
as Truth, Peace, Charity, Faith, and Friendship)
reflect the influence of Father Samuel Mazzuchelli,
who, back in the 1800s, thought that it wouldn't hurt
to remind the rowdy miners of this area of a few biblical virtues.*

*For insight into the miners' lives, you can visit an
1827 hand-dug lead mine and experience the small
spaces and rugged working conditions. No wonder
they acted out after a twelve-hour day down there.
The Badger Mine and Museum are at the village park
on West Estey Street, open daily from 10:00 A.M. to
4:00 P.M., Memorial Day through Labor Day. Call
(608) 965–4860 for more information.*

S UN   C ITY
S o l d i e r s   G r o v e

Soldiers Grove, population 564, looks different from other towns and villages in Crawford County. Buildings in the business district on the south end of town have rooftop collectors and skylights, and its streets have names like Solar Circle, Passive Sun Drive, and Sunbeam Boulevard. It is the first, and possibly the only, solar village in the United States.

After enduring several major floods, the people of Soldiers Grove had had it up to here with the Kickapoo River, and they had the highwater marks all up and down Main Street to prove it. Rowing down Main Street wasn't funny anymore, and pumping out the basement never had been. After another major flood on the Fourth of July weekend in 1978, they took the high road: Instead of trying to control the river with dams and levees, they decided to move Soldiers Grove to higher ground. And while they were solving problems, such as the local economy, they adopted an ordinance that required new buildings to use the sun for at least half their heating needs. A study in 1991 concluded that the buildings are cost-effective.

Soldiers Grove is on County Highway 131 in the northeast corner of Crawford County.

WHERE GIANT SOMBREROS COME FROM
Sparta

If you like the miniature landmarks in Pardeeville (page 161), you might want to cross over to the other side of the looking glass by stopping at the headquarters of FAST (Fiberglass Animals, Shapes and Trademarks). Outside are clues to the projects that take place in the workshop: colossal roosters, cheeseburgers, ice cream cones, pumpkins, hobos, frogs.

FAST specializes in making gigantic landmarks and trademarks. It has probably made your favorite, whether it's the 50-foot-tall Jolly Green Giant in Blue Earth, Minnesota; the

FAST, home of all creatures great and gargantuan.

world's largest killer bee, in Hidalgo, Texas; or the 200-foot sombrero in South Carolina. Not to mention many of those chickens and clowns at fast-food places.

Even abroad you can't miss FAST's work: the 26-foot pirate in Japan or the massive gorilla on a hillside in Colombia, where you stand in its chest and survey the water park below through a telescope. Furthermore, since fiberglass lasts forever, your great-great-great-great-grandchildren will be admiring all these things, too.

By the way, if you object to the 8-foot monkey holding a 7-foot banana that sprays water from each end and appeared in your neighbor's yard late last year, here's good news: It disappeared en route to its intended destination and FAST is offering a reward for its return.

FAST is located on Highway 21 East just outside of Sparta. It sells a catalog that's a hoot, too. Call (608) 269–7110 for more information.

T*HE* H*OUSE OF A* G*UY'S* O*WN*
S*pring* G*reen*

The House on the Rock is just a wee bit overdone. The carousel, for instance, has 20,000 lights, 182 chandeliers, 269 creatures (but not a single horse), and hundreds of mannequin-angels hovering and rotating overhead. There also are 250 dollhouses, miniature circuses with more than a million pieces, an organ console with fifteen keyboards, and tons of everything. At Christmas there are 6,000 Santas.

A tour of the extraordinary sixteen-building complex is like a movie made with a handheld camera. Is this room moving? The mix of music coming from all directions adds to the confusion, and together it has the quality of high school band practice.

By the time you stagger out three or four hours later, it's hard to name the strangest sight: The bushy eyebrows of a Fu Manchu drummer keeping time to "Danse Macabre" in the two-story Mikado exhibit? The carrying case for a woman's artificial leg, inlaid with a Derringer pistol, in Unique Weaponry? The soaring pipes, catwalks, and massive machinery in the cavelike Organ Room, to the tune of the "Anniversary Waltz"? The curious tableaux taking place within the dollhouses? The plaintive sight of an empty little rowboat in the jaw of the 200-foot sea creature in the six-story Heritage of the Sea? Ronald Reagan in the trumpet section of the life-size, eighty-piece, automated circus orchestra?

The tour opens in the Japanese-style stone house that Alex Jordan began building in the 1940s. Then in his thirties, Jordan was a job-hopping, ex-student, ex–cab driver from Madi-

Circus musicians at House on the Rock wear Dodgeville High School band uniforms.

son. He favored low ceilings, dim lighting, carpeted surfaces instead of furniture, and fireplaces. To add to the seductive effect, a phantom chamber orchestra of bows saws away at Ravel's "Bolero." Several more such rooms lead to daylight and the Infinity Room, a 218-foot, glass-walled, cantilevered structure that soars out over the Wyoming Valley and offers a view of the valley floor, fifteen stories straight down.

The "expansion phase" represents Jordan's eccentric obsession to collect the largest, the biggest, and the most of whatever he came across—dolls, clocks, violins, mirrors, paperweights, weapons—and a place to put it all. Jordan never had enough of anything, and what he couldn't collect, he created. "It doesn't have to be good, it doesn't have to be bad, it just has to be," he often said. Much of what is here came from the on-site workshop.

The House on the Rock is one of Wisconsin's most mind-boggling and popular attractions. Open daily from mid-March to the last weekend in October, 9:00 A.M. to 7:00 P.M. during the spring and fall, to 8:00 P.M. Memorial Day to Labor Day. Christmas season lasts for about eight weeks, until New Year's. On Highway 23 between Spring Green and Dodgeville. Admission charge. Call (608) 935–3639 or visit www. houseontherock.com for details.

So That's What Happened
to Anne Baxter
Spring Green

Now why would a tree in honor of Hollywood actress Anne Baxter (1924–1986) be growing in this rural cemetery, next to Unity Chapel? Because it's the Lloyd Jones family burial ground, and her mother, Catherine Wright Baxter, was architect Frank Lloyd Wright's first daughter, and Wright's mother was one of the "God-almighty Joneses," as the neighbors called them, for their highmindedness and tendency to preside over the countryside ("Truth against the world" was the family motto). Anne Baxter played such roles as Eve Harrington in *All About Eve* ("If nothing else, there's applause . . . like waves of love pouring over the footlights"), a princess of the Nile in *The Ten Commandments* ("Oh, Moses, you stubborn, splendid, adorable fool!"), and later on, for fun, Olga, Queen of the Cossacks, in several "Batman" episodes.

Frank Lloyd Wright's gravestone is here, but it marks an empty grave. He was buried here in 1959, but when his widow, Olgivanna, died in 1985, his body was removed and cremated so that his ashes could join hers at Taliesin West in Arizona, as her will specified.

The cemetery is 3 miles south of Spring Green, on County Highway T, east of Highway 23.

FIRST, SOAK ONE MOUNTAIN
Trempealeau

Trempealeau Mountain rises out of the Mississippi River just north of town. Appropriately enough, the name means "mountain soaking in water." It's a solid-rock island, the tallest of three island-mountains along the Mississippi.

The mountain was an important landmark for early steamboat pilots. Today river travelers are more likely to think of this point in the river as Lock and Dam Number 6, one of five on the Wisconsin side.

Lockmaster is not a job for your basic Type A personality. It takes about two hours for a towboat to maneuver a barge through the locks—if all goes well—and five days for the 669-mile trip between Saint Paul and Saint Louis. Picture yourself

sharing the highway with the fifty-eight trucks it would take
to transport the same amount of cargo and give the barge captain a big smile.

You can watch the action from an observation tower
between the Mississippi and the railroad tracks that run paral-
lel to the river. Apparently this is a principal north–south
route; freight trains roar through here about every thirty or
forty minutes. A biking and hiking trail is also nearby. All in
all, this would be a good place for scouts to work on their
Transportation badge.

THE GARDEN OF EDEN

*You can't have missed the fact, thanks to J. Heile-
man Brewing, that Wisconsin is God's Country,
but did you know it also was the site of the Garden
of Eden? According to the Reverend D. O. Van Slyke
of Galesville, his own Trempealeau County along the
Mississippi matched the biblical description perfectly—four rivers, surrounding bluffs, hanging
gardens, milk, honey, apples, and plenty of snakes,
albeit rattle.*

*Van Slyke was a circuit-riding preacher whose
ministry included spreading the word about the discovery of Eden at the confluence of Highways 53 and
54 and drawing the faithful back to the state of inno-
cence. His 1886 pamphlet "Garden of Eden" made the
case for the Wisconsin Eden, suggesting that Adam
and Eve, having fallen from grace, moved to Minnesota (say, the Twin Cities—Sodom and Gomorrah?).*

You're in Good Hands with Hüpeden
Valton

The community of Valton consists of just a handful of scattered buildings, and one of them is remarkable. On the outside, simple: white frame, 60 by 24 feet. On the inside, busy: every square inch is covered with a panoramic mural portraying the rituals and activities of the Modern Woodmen of America, a fraternal insurance society that flourished here around 1900.

It is the work of an itinerant landscape painter, Ernst Hüpeden, who arrived in Valton in 1897 and was hired to paint the stage curtain for the Woodmen Meeting Hall. The Woodmen were so pleased and impressed with the Mississippi River scene he produced that they asked him to continue. He agreed, in exchange for room and board and drink, according to one account of his life, which describes Hüpeden as "a colorful, tragic figure" whose past included emptying and painting whiskey bottles.

He went on to paint vivid scenes set in a pine forest that are both frightening depictions of injury and death (and life without life insurance?) and peaceful depictions of home life and fellowship among Woodmen. One scene shows a woman in mourning dress cashing in her insurance policy. Another reveals a curious initiation rite that involved strapping new members to a wooden goat on wheels and rolling them around the hall.

The Kohler Foundation funded the restoration of the Painted Forest, which is located a block north of County Highway EE at Sixth and Painted Forest Drive. It is open between 1:00 and 3:30 P.M. on Saturday in June, July, and August. To arrange to view it at other times, call (608) 983–2352.

CRANBERRY COMPETITION BOGS DOWN
Warrens

The annual Biggest Cranberry Contest is part of the three-day Warrens Cranberry Festival. Entries are judged by weight in grams. In case of a tie, the berries are measured for overall length, configuration, and originality of presentation to determine the winner.

Blue ribbons are awarded in ten different classes of cranberries. "Biggest Cranberry of Show" receives $25. ("Biggest" in 1999 weighed 5.33 grams. If that fails to impress you, weigh a few cranberries and read that line again.) Cranberries are displayed until the end of the festival on Sunday.

Wisconsin ranks first in U.S. cranberry production, and the Warrens gathering in late September is the largest cranberry festival in the world. It includes a parade, a fall produce market, several miles of antiques and crafts, bus tours of cranberry marshes, and even cranberry royalty—little tiny red round people with regal bearing. Festival information is available at www.cranfest.com or (608) 378–4200.

A LIVING FLAG
Witwen

The little community of Witwen consists of about twenty houses that face one another along two-lane Highway E. But neighbors come from miles around for Witwen's Fourth of July Parade. Lining up along the south edge of town, they point their vans toward the cornfields, pop their hatches, and set up lawn chairs behind the white line.

A preteen brass band plays "This Is My Country," the Busy Badgers and the Happy Hustlers 4-H Clubs toss candy from their floats, and a great deal of farm machinery rolls by. But the high point of the parade is the Living Flag, a row of seven women marching shoulder to shoulder, dressed in satin robes that line up to form Old Glory. The tradition was started almost fifty years ago.

The women who march today are members of the Sauk County Homemakers. They occasionally appear at other Wisconsin events, parades, or centennial celebrations. (But not if it looks like rain. Raindrops ruin satin.) They've been featured in the national media ever since Charles Kuralt discovered them "On the Road" in 1980, and they appear in Kuralt's video "Seasons of America."

Witwen is 7 miles west of Sauk City. The parade begins around 10:00 or 10:30 A.M.

"She's a Grand Old Flag . . . " The Living Flag of Sauk County.

INDEX

HELP US KEEP THIS GUIDE UP TO DATE

Every effort has been made by the authors and editors to make this guide as accurate and useful as possible. However, many things can change after a guide is published—establishments close, phone numbers change, facilities come under new management, and so forth.

We would love to hear from you concerning your experiences with this guide and how you feel it could be made better and kept up to date. While we may not be able to respond directly to your comments and suggestions, we'll take them to heart and we'll also make certain to share them with the authors. Please send your comments and suggestions to the following address:

> The Globe Pequot Press
> Reader Response/Editorial Department
> P.O. Box 480
> Guilford, CT 06437

Or you may e-mail us at:

> editorial@globe-pequot.com

Thanks for your input, and happy travels!

ABOUT THE AUTHORS

Michael Feldman has been doing radio for the better or worse part of twenty years, most of it spent producing and hosting Michael Feldman's *Whad'Ya Know?* on Public Radio International. He lives in Madison, Wisconsin, with one wife, Sandy, two daughters, Ellie and Nora, and a yellow lab, Sugar.

Diana Cook painstakingly researches the questions but not the answers for Michael Feldman's *Whad'Ya Know?* and does freelance editorial work in Madison. She is the author of *Wisconsin Capitol: Fascinating Facts* and contributes to *The Wisconsin Almanac*. She's also the mother of Andrew and Julia.